# My healthcare is killing me!

a personal journal

## JULIE KLEIN

My Healthcare Is Killing Me!

## Acknowledgments:

I want to thank everyone who believed my story was worth telling before I did.

Most of all I want to thank Leslie Cedar. Without you, this book would never have happened. From the day you asked to read some of my journal notes, to the endless months of editing when you knew I was too weak and tired to do it alone, you have always been my champion and my guardian angel.

To my many editors who looked past my atrocious punctuation because they also believed in me,

I treasure you all:

Jennifer, Leslie, Jimi, Charlotte, Gloria, Mark

To my wonderful mother who has always felt I was born to write. I love you mom, I could never have survived those awful years of illness without being able to fall completely apart with you.

To my fiancé George, I know I am not the same person you first fell in love with, but thank you for never making me feel that it mattered. Your love and support never wavered, even when I felt impossible to love.

# "**Write** what should not be **forgotten**...."

Isabel Allende

It is an absolute miracle that I am alive today, not only because I was diagnosed with two aggressive cancers in a row, but because I survived the shocking realities of our healthcare system.

*Here is my story:*

# CHAPTER ONE

# What's that lump?

## January 3, 2008

7:00: a.m. I wake up emotionally paralyzed, unable to perform my morning rituals.

7:15: I do not have my usual morning coffee.

7:30: I do not brush my teeth.

7:45: I do not shower.

8:00: I sit on my bed, huddled in a fetal position with my cell phone in my hand, waiting for my doctor's call.

Time ...Creeps....Agonizingly...By...

Each minute I wait becomes more and more unbearable. George, my fiancé, out of habit, leans over and kisses my forehead, "Have a nice day."

"When I find out the results, do you want me to just leave it on your voice mail?"

"Yes."

I pop another Xanax, realizing I am emotionally alone in my terror. Perhaps he feels it too but just can't show it.

8:15

8:30

9:00: I am popping Xanax like M&M's— *these .025 mg are useless!*

9:15:   *Would a glass of wine help? I never drink in the morning.*
        *Well, maybe the occasional mimosa at a wedding.*

9:30

10:00

10:15: *So this is how it feels to lose my mind.*

10:30: I pour another glass of wine to try to keep myself from
        falling into the abyss.

I drift back to what happened over the last three months...

◄——◇——►

*I found a lump in my breast in early October, 2007. Not just
any lump...a hard, jagged, golf- ball sized, foreign object that I
instinctively knew did not belong in my body. I was not ready to
cope, so I lived in denial for a few weeks, assuring myself I had
been drinking way too much coffee. When it became impossible to
ignore, I saw Dr. King, my gynecologist. He examined me and felt
the lump, then urged me to go for a mammogram and sonogram
immediately. He tried to reassure me,"It moves, so it's probably just
a cyst, but let's follow-up to make sure."*

*After getting the mammogram and sonogram on December 10,
Dr. King referred me to Dr. Rodriguez, who specializes in breast
cancer. When I met him, he was very calm and soft- spoken. He
promised that in spite of the holiday, we would move the process
along, as he realized how unnerving waiting for results can be.*

*On December 17th, I received a call from my gynecologist's office,
"You'd better get off the estrogen you are taking! You'll be getting a
call tomorrow with the results of the sonogram."*

UH-OH!

*The next day I waited all morning for a phone call that never came.
Unable to function from anxiety, I called Dr. Rodriguez's office about*

11:45 a.m. and spoke with an insensitive, apathetic receptionist.

"You have a biopsy at eight o'clock."

"I do? Nobody told me this? Where do I go at eight o'clock?"

"No no!" she scolded me. "Eight o'clock on the breast!"

There is an awkward silence while I try to decipher what she is talking about.

"Oh! Do you mean that eight o'clock is the location on my breast where the biopsy will be performed?" I felt the need to sarcastically clarify, just to let her know that patients shouldn't have to solve biopsy word puzzles!

"Yes." she responded with impatience.

"Okay. Where do I go for the biopsy?"

Later that evening, I told George about my day. He has kept a calendar on the kitchen wall as a way of keeping track of important events in our lives. He had a marker in his hand and was ready to document the date of my biopsy appointment but the medical jargon was new to him. Being deaf in one ear, sometimes he mixes up certain unfamiliar words. He innocently asked me, "What date is your autopsy again?"

"Honey, I think you mean biopsy not autopsy?" We nervously joked about this all night.

About a week after the biopsy, useless, alarming phone calls from Dr. Rodrigues's staff began… The first call:

"Hi, Julie, How are you?"

"I'm not doing so well, I'm a wreck. What are my results?"

"Dr. Rodriguez will be calling you on Thursday. I am just calling to see how you are feeling after the biopsy."

I think to myself: How am I feeling? How does she think I'm feeling, I am waiting for a call to determine if I have cancer. Every time the office calls, my heart drops and I feel sick to my stomach. Wouldn't you think a doctor's office that deals with biopsies and cancer would be a little more sensitive about the terror I am feeling waiting for the results?

Another call:

"Hi, is this Julie Klein?"

"Yes, it's Julie Klein. Am I dying? Do I have cancer? Has it spread? Will I need chemo? Will I lose my hair?"

She answers in slow motion, "Hi, Julie...how... are ...you...? This is the nurse's assistant from Dr. Rodriguez's office. I have your results in front of me and the doctor will be calling you tomorrow morning to discuss them."

I anxiously asked, "What are my results? Is it cancer?"

"Oh, I can't tell you that—I would lose my job."

"Wait a minute...you mean to tell me that you have the results in front of you. You know if I have cancer, and if so, how bad it is, and you're not going to tell me?"

"I'm sorry, I'm not allowed."

"Then why are you calling me again?"

The child's song runs through my head, "I know something you don't know...nah nah nah nah nah nah!" I try to wrap my brain around the sadistic person who instituted this policy. Let's see, how can we make this patient's suffering and waiting even more excruciating? Wouldn't it be fun to torment her by implying something is terribly wrong, her life may be in jeopardy, but we instituted an important policy that prevents us from disclosing the details. Perhaps if we make her wait in this panicky state long enough, she will have a heart attack or stroke first, then we won't have to deliver the bad news about her cancer diagnosis!

She reiterates,"I know how you feel, people get upset with me all the time. I wish I could tell you. He will call you tomorrow morning."

"I will be assuming the worst until I hear from the doctor— can *he please please call me as early as possible? Promise me I will be his first call in the morning?"*

"He will call you first thing tomorrow morning, I promise." I sense a glimmer of compassion in her voice. I hang up the phone and start to shake with fear.

---

10:45: **Finally!** The phone rings and jars me back to reality.

"Hi, may I please talk to Julie Klein."

"Yes. Yes. This is Julie. Do I have cancer?" My heart is beating so fast that my pajama top is visibly fluttering.

"Hi, this is Brittany from Dr. Rodriguez's office; he wants you to come in later this afternoon for a consultation."

"You have got to be kidding! I am in no condition to drive. Put the doctor on the phone now!"

Surprisingly, she listens to my command and within a minute I hear Dr. Rodriguez's voice, "Hello, Julie, I need you to come to my downtown office this afternoon at 3:30 to discuss your results."

*I don't think so! Game over. I've had enough!*

"Dr. Rodriguez, with all due respect, I am in no condition to drive, I've had two glasses of wine and two Xanax waiting for your call. I am imagining myself with no hair and no breasts… or worse! What is it that you can't tell me that I am not already assuming?" Before he answers me, he feels the need to warn me about mixing Xanax and alcohol.

"I know, I know, I never mix, particularly before noon, but I'm a little freaked-out right now!" I am annoyed having to explain why I find it necessary to numb myself at this particular juncture. I think of negotiating with him, *"How about if I promise never to mix Xanax and alcohol again if you promise to keep your insensitive twelve-year old employees away from the biopsy patients!* Instead I beg, "Please, please, please can't you just tell me the results now?"

He takes pity on me and acquiesces. He clinically recites:

"You have a malignancy. It is 1.7 centimeters. You have Invasive Ductal Carcinoma, the most common form of breast cancer. It is considered small and very treatable. You must come to my downtown office this afternoon to discuss treatment options."

"Thank you, doctor, I will see you this afternoon." I catch a glimpse of my expression in the mirror and see a stranger staring back at me. For the rest of my life I will now be a cancer "survivor." In my surreal fog, I have two phone calls to make— George and my parents.

First, I call George. His voice-mail answers so I do as instructed earlier that morning, "Hi. It's me. It's cancer. It is considered very treatable. I am on my way to Dr. Rodriguez's office now to find out more. Love you."

On a very profound level, I don't understand why he is not picking up the phone right now! What on earth could be more important? I put on a brave face and tell myself that men are just very different than women.

Hopefully he will redeem himself, but not today.

My next call is to my parents. My only sibling died in 1999 from a genetic form of muscular dystrophy, making this call even more heartbreaking. How do I simultaneously convey that I have cancer while also conveying that I will be okay? Our small family has definitely faced hardship before, I just don't want to be the embodiment of a new dread. I am supposed to be the lucky one, the winner of the random genetic lottery.

In our family I was never the one my parents worried about.

My brother was one year older, yet, everything was so much harder for him…school, making friends, dates, career success. By comparison, it all came so easily to me. There wasn't a day without mixed feelings for my dear, frail brother… gratitude and sorrow, relief and guilt. I was fiercely protective of him, and a palpable sadness was alway in my heart.

I lived with the knowledge that I was a few genes away from a devastating illness. If I had been born first, I may have ended up in a wheelchair. I have lived with this awareness my entire life, a burden and a blessing in one confused mind.

From the outside looking in, it didn't appear as though I was more exceptional than any other kid my age. I was attractive, but not beautiful. I was intelligent, but not a genius. I was average, but far from ordinary. Perhaps my closeness to my brother made me a very sensitive soul who could feel everyone else's pain. Being too young to process all of this emotion, I became odd.

I was happiest spending hours alone in my room. It was my sanctuary. I would read books about nonconformity like **The Catcher in the Rye** and listen to music that seemed to express my pain. I was mesmerized by Ralph Waldo Emerson and Henry David Thoreau's **Civil Disobedience**. In my teenage mind I arrogantly thought I had invented nonconformity. This made it so fascinating to read about others who had lived many decades before me and had struggled with the same issues. My true friends were Justin Haywood from the Moody Blues, Holden Caulfield, and, of course, Betty Friedan and Gloria Steinem.

I was repelled by normal.

I remember the nice Jewish boy who lived next door and had a crush on me. His family had us married off with two kids and a dog. The thought of that life felt suffocating to me.

I was more drawn to people who were deep, dark and conflicted. The curious thing about my oddness was that I could hide it. I could pass for mainstream; I looked like the girl- next -door, but deep down I knew that life was hard and not always fair.

---·---→

My parents live about twenty minutes away. As soon as they hear my news, they rush over to our condo and insist on driving me to Dr. Rodriguez's downtown office. I am so grateful not to face this alone.

When we get there, there are signs all over the institutional gray walls that proclaim "BEAT CANCER." I would have had a nervous breakdown if I hadn't dragged the diagnosis out of Dr. Rodriguez earlier and known my case is highly treatable. The logic of not telling patients over the phone completely escapes me. Why on earth would doctors think it's better to send their patients blindly into a cancer facility rather than just telling them over the phone? Boy, when I recover, I want to have a little chat with Dr. Rodriguez about his policies and procedures!

In my moment of horror, I play out this injustice in my mind as if I had followed instructions and been a "good patient."

*I would have gotten the call from the assistant saying that she couldn't discuss the results. I would have obeyed her instructions and waited until 3:30 not knowing if I was going to survive, somehow keeping it together enough to get myself to the downtown office.*

Upon entering the office, I would be shocked and traumatized to clearly see that this is a major cancer facility. Not knowing my own diagnosis or prognosis, I would be completely unprepared for this. In the waiting room I would see numerous cancer patients, a pale woman with no hair and another woman with one of those hideous, terry-cloth cancer beanies on her head. To my left I would see the small room where skeletal figures are hooked up to IV's. I would have nervously waited in the lobby thinking I was dying until the doctor finally called me into his office at 4:30 pm.

*Are you kidding me?*

*Who on earth but a delusional person would be able to come out of that scenario unscathed? Knowing my case was highly treatable before going to that facility was the only thing that saved my sanity!*

As we wait, I whisper the obvious to my parents, "I guess that's where people get chemo."

When I finally see Dr. Rodriguez, I want to make a better impression than I had earlier that morning over the phone so he won't send me to rehab before my cancer treatment! I make a concentrated effort to be as mature, intelligent and articulate as possible. I hang onto every word he says and take very specific notes.

Apparently I have a choice, either a lumpectomy or a mastectomy. Chemo will be a decision made by my team which consists of an oncologist, radiologist and Dr. Rodriguez, my surgeon. The next step is a breast MRI and a PET scan to see if I have any other cancer in my body. His office schedules an MRI for January 9th and tells me to come back here to this cancer facility to have the test. I like him, but something he says disturbs me, **"If you are the type of person who will be nervous every time you have your yearly mammogram, you may as well have a mastectomy."**

# CHAPTER 2

## Delays Delays Delays

**January 8, 2008**

Dr. Rodriguez's receptionist calls this morning and asks, "Where do you want to have your MRI?"

I snap back, "What do you mean? I thought I was scheduled to have it at your downtown location tomorrow. They made the appointment when I was just there a few days ago."

Confused, she replies, "That's weird. We don't even have an MRI machine."

"What is going on? I plead, "I am going to call right now to straighten this out!"

My hands are shaking with anxiety as I call the downtown facility where I am supposed to have the MRI the next day. They explain to me that they do not have an MRI machine and the appointment I have scheduled is actually for a consultation with an oncologist.

*For the first time, I begin to question if I am in capable hands.*

"This is news to me. I thought the appointment was for an MRI."

"No, this is a consultation with an oncologist."

"I don't understand, don't I need the MRI and PET scan **before** the consultation?"

"Well, at this point it doesn't matter because this appointment isn't covered by your insurance anyway. What do you want to do about the appointment for the consultation?"

I reply, "You might as well cancel it. I need an oncologist that takes my insurance."

At my whits end, frantic and overwhelmed, I call my gynecologist's office for guidance, explaining that I urgently need to speak with Dr. King. He calls me back within an hour.

"Dr. King, I am getting very concerned about my care. I like Dr. Rodriguez, but I feel like I am getting the run-around with his office. Over a month has gone by since my biopsy and I still haven't had an MRI and I can't find an oncologist that takes my insurance."

He sounds concerned. "No, No, that doesn't sound right. You should have had surgery by now to remove the cancer." He gives me the name of another breast surgeon and wishes me well.

He must have immediately called Dr. Rodriguez because just as I was scheduling the appointment for the second opinion, Dr. Rodriguez, himself, calls me, which is highly unusual. I only get calls from his staff. He is reassuring and professional. "Julie, we do this all of the time. I can see why it seems like things are taking a long time, but I assure you everything is progressing as it should."

"Dr. Rodriguez, I am really happy to hear from you. I am getting very worried that my treatment is taking so long to get started. I don't have an MRI scheduled yet. I thought I was going tomorrow, but I just found out that the appointment was actually for a consultation with an oncologist. That had to be cancelled because the oncologist didn't even take my insurance. What is going on with your office?"

He calmly explains he will have them straighten everything

out. He gives me the name of a designated office manager for my contact point, her name is Pat. "If you have any more roadblocks, you can talk to her."

Pat promptly calls me back with the name of another oncologist who definitely takes my insurance and she schedules my MRI appointment for me. She explains that I just need to call my primary doctor's office to get the referrals from my insurance company.

In the meantime, I am in a panic that my treatment is taking so long to get started. I feel like these delays are causing my cancer to spread and reproduce like fruit flies. I desperately start googling "holistic cures for cancer" and read about this juice called "Pom Wonderful" that is full of antioxidants that may help prevent cancer from spreading.

It would be "pom wonderful" if I could actually get treated with chemo and surgery! I feel so completely helpless with these idiotic delays that I have to do **something** to save myself, so I buy a ton of this stuff and guzzle it every chance I get!

### January 17, 2008

I get a call from my primary doctor's office, "Julie, The second oncologist that Dr. Rodriguez's office is recommending is not on your insurance either."

"This is not possible, they just looked it up for me a few days ago."

"I don't know what to tell you, your insurance is denying it."

Upset at the constant roadblocks, I call my insurance company.

"Hello, I am having trouble finding an oncologist in my area, can you give me a few names please."

Jason, the insurance representative, agrees to help. I hear him flipping through pages mumbling, "I don't see any in your area."

"Jason, I don't understand. This can't be, I live in an area with a lot of retired people, this doesn't make any sense."

"Sorry, but I'm looking at the directory and this is what it says... Oh wait, here's a name for you."

He gives me a name and address.

"Jason, that is more than two hours from my home!"

"I don't know what to tell you."

In frustration and anger, I hang up the phone.

It is becoming increasingly more difficult for me to remain calm. I call back Dr. Rodriguez's office and ask for Pat, "Help! The doctor you gave me isn't on my insurance plan either! I just spoke to the insurance representative and he told me that the nearest oncologist is over two hours away!"

Pat is shocked and insistent. "Something is very wrong here. I am going to call your insurance company myself. Do you want to hold for me or have me call you back?"

"I'll hold."

I grab another large bottle of Pom Wonderful and frantically guzzle it down. Pat gets back on the line, "Julie, you will never believe what happened. Your insurance company was looking under O for Oncologist. Most Oncologists are filed under H for Hematology/Oncology.

"You have got to be kidding me!"

"You should be okay now. I've made an appointment with an oncologist in your area on January 25th. You just need to pick up the referral at your primary care doctor's office."

"Thank you, thank you, thank you!"

## January 25, 2008

As my friend Gail and I enter the oncology office we are bombarded by the pungent smell of harsh, potent chemicals. Immediately, on our right, is a small room where the nurses skillfully take about three vials of my blood then send me back to the main waiting room. We then wait **almost three hours** before my name is called to see my new oncologist.

As we look around the room, I whisper to Gail, "Everyone still has hair."

A wave of giddy hope rushes through me. Maybe chemo has come a long way and I won't lose my hair.

I ask the first person I meet, Tanya, the nurse. "How come everyone has hair in the waiting room?"

She touches my hand and smiles gently, leaning in and whispering,

"Look again."

I was in disbelief, "No way! Wigs? "

"Yep."

Tanya has a razor sharp bluntness that I find refreshing. Her no-nonsense approach makes me feel that I am going to be okay. There is something comforting about the staff's lack of alarm. My case is ordinary to them.

"What kind of cancer you got?"

"Breast"

She pointed to my shirt and asked, "You gonna lose them?"

I reply in the same blunt staccato, "Not sure, hope not"

She explains to Gail and me that the doctor is running behind today, so we should make ourselves comfortable in the lobby. My friend Gail has been so wonderful. She went through breast cancer several years back. From the beginning of my journey, she explained to me everything that I will be facing from a human perspective, not a clinical one. When I express to Gail how grateful I am for her help during this tough time, she tells me about the "girl code." She will do everything she can to help get me through my cancer, then I have to agree to pay it forward and help the next woman

I know who is diagnosed with this awful disease. I love this idea! However, I am sure she is reconsidering this plan as we approach our third hour in the waiting room!

We are finally escorted to a small cubicle and told, "The doctor will be right with you." My oncologist barges into the room, unapologetic about the long wait. She is around my age, in her late forties. She is tall and thin with dark hair. Her perfect bob hairstyle angles just beneath her chin, reminding me of some of the cold female executives I worked with in my prior corporate life. I can see that she is well-dressed under her white lab coat. As she shuffles through my records, she appears unprepared. Perhaps the long nervous wait is affecting my opinion of her, but I don't feel like we are "clicking."

She bluntly explains that the MRI report indicates that the tumor is much larger than originally thought. It is now 3.4 cm. not 1.7 cm as Dr. Rodriguez had originally advised me. *I can't help wondering if all of those delays with my insurance company and Dr. Rodriguez's office have something to do with the tumor doubling in size.* She explains that I will have four rounds of very strong chemo, first to shrink the tumor before surgery, then 12 more rounds of a less potent chemo after the surgery.

"You will need to have a series of tests to make sure your heart is strong enough to withstand the chemo. You will need an EKG and a test called a Muga scan." She then takes out a calendar and circles February 8th for my first chemo treatment. She continues to study the pictures of my tumor which are displayed on the wall. Pointing to the area of the tumor, she is mumbling, "mastectomy, yes, yes, mastectomy," as if Gail and I are not in the room.

In a panic I blurt out, "I'm having a lumpectomy, right?"

"That's the plan."

"Then why did you just say I need a mastectomy?"

"Oh, I was just thinking you would definitely need a mastectomy if you were not having the chemo first to shrink the tumor."

"Dr., I am the type of person who will replay this conversation in my mind at 2 o'clock in the morning and believe that I heard you say I need a mastectomy, so I need you to confirm that the plan of treatment is a lumpectomy."

"Yes, that is the plan as long as the chemo works to shrink the tumor."

"What are the chances that it won't work?"

"It should, but there are no guarantees."

*I am really trying to like her. It took me so long to find an oncologist that takes my insurance, I **need** to like her. So far, it's not working. Her caustic demeanor scares me.*

### January 28th 2008

I get a call from the hospital today, "Hello, may I please speak with Julie Klein."

"Speaking."

"Hi, Julie." We are calling to let you know that your insurance company is not authorizing your heart test tomorrow."

"Are you kidding me? Why?"

"I don't know, you will have to ask **them**."

Exasperated, I dial my insurance company ready to explode.

"Hello. May I please speak to a supervisor immediately."

"Please hold."

"This is John. How can I help you today."

"John, I have cancer, *I feel my blood boiling,* I need a test called a Muga scan to see if my heart is strong enough to withstand the chemo treatment. My test is being denied by your company and I want to know why."

"Let me look into that for you. Please hold."

John comes back on the line about fifteen minutes later, " You can't have the test done at the hospital."

"Why not?"

"You need to have the test done at a free-standing building."

"I don't know what you are talking about."

"You can have the test, you just can't have the test at a location that is in any way affiliated with, or attached to, a hospital or clinic. That is what is meant by a free-standing building."

I feel rage, "Why?"

"It costs more."

"You are joking!" I reach for another bottle of Pom Wonderful to wash down my Xanax.

"I can give you a few numbers of other facilities, but you will have to call and see if they are free-standing."

"Let me get this straight, my cancer is reproducing rapidly as we speak, and I have to waste time calling facility after facility asking them about their architecture? (I take another swig of Pom Wonderful.) Can't you do this for me?"

"I'm pretty busy, it would probably be faster if you did it yourself."

I slam the phone down so hard it almost breaks!

A number of frustrating days go by before I find "free-standing buildings" for my Muga scan, and PET scan. I am getting worried that I won't have enough time to get the results of these tests to my oncologist before my first treatment on February 8th.

## February 7th, 2008

Despite my best efforts to try to get all of my tests before tomorrow, I am unable to do so. As a result, my first chemo must be postponed.

# CHAPTER 3

# Learning New Vocabulary Words

**February 15, 2008**

Now that all of the insurance delays have pushed my care back by almost three months, it is finally time for my long-awaited chemo. George is being so sweet and supportive. I know how difficult it is for him to get the day off from work, but he really wants to come with me for my first treatment. Shortly after we arrive at my oncologist's office, I am called into the nursing station to have my blood drawn. I see my buddy, Tanya, the nurse and I instantly feel calmer.

"Hey Julie! How you doin' girl? You ready for your first chemo?"

"I think so."

She smiles and nods, then asks,

"Hey… you gotta man?"

"Yeah…in the lobby"

"I'm gonna tell you what I tell all my breast cancer ladies. You sit his ass down and tell him, 'Look, this ain't gonna be pretty. This is gonna get real rough. I don't want you saying you can handle this, then three-maybe four- months down the road you come to me all whiny and say, 'I can't take this anymore.' If you ain't in it for the long hall…I want your ass out now!"

I immediately love her fierce protectiveness of her patients, even though her concerns about George are unfounded.

"He's in the waiting room, you wanna meet him?"

She follows me to where my wonderful, sweet George is nervously waiting for me, takes one look into his worried eyes and everything about her softens.

"You gonna take care of our girl, aren't ya?"

Somewhat confused, he plays along, "Of course."

Tanya gently places her hand on George's shoulder and instructs us to wait until my name is called. "Your doctor is running behind so it might be a while."

As we wait, we are under the impression that I will be going right into the "chemo room" to start my treatment. Instead, George and I are escorted to a private room. After waiting for another half-hour, my oncologist rushes in and announces, "You may not be able to have chemo. There is a problem with your heart."

"What?"

"The results of your Muga scan came back inconclusive."

*I can't believe what I am hearing. This feels like a nightmare. I have cancer and a bad heart? This must be a mistake, they must have me mixed up with someone else. I really thought I was a healthy person? I eat right, I exercise, I'm not overweight, I don't smoke?*

Thank God George remembers that there was a problem with the "free standing building" where I had the Muga scan. I had the test on February 7th, then the facility called me a few days later and told me I had to re-take the test because the machine was broken. I wasn't too thrilled about that since the test made me so radioactive that I had to be quarantined from the waiting room. I had to sit in isolation for thirty minutes while this toxic dye ran through my nervous system!

George explains this to my oncologist who I have now nick-named Dr. Scary. She mutters, "Oh, that might explain it," as she starts to exit out of the room.

I stop her before she runs out the door, "Doctor, (my voice is quivering with terror) can you find out if my biopsy results came back? I have been too afraid to call for the results myself. Did my cancer spread? Are my lymph nodes involved? It has been over a week but I was too paralyzed with fear to call."

"Let me find out."

She leaves the room for so long I wonder if she decides to go on an impromptu vacation. When she comes back in the room she declares, "I have some auspicious news."

I can't read her deadpan expression, and I can't recall what auspicious means.

Getting results of your biopsy at the oncologist's office is not the optimum time to learn new vocabulary words. I search every inch of her face looking for some indication whether I am going to live or die. Her face reveals nothing.

I think to myself: *auspicious, auspicious…is that good or bad? It kind of sounded like foreboding. It sounds bad. Really really bad. SHIT I am going to die! OH MY GOD, the results of my biopsy are auspicious!*

I look at George and want to scream at the top of my lungs, "What the hell does auspicious mean?"

It takes every ounce of self-control for me to be diplomatic.

"I'm sorry, doctor, the meaning of the word auspicious seems to have escaped me. Is the news good or bad?"

She looks at me with a forced, condescending smile and says, "Good. Auspicious is good. Your heart is fine and your cancer did not spread to the lymph nodes. You can start chemo today."

*Would it have killed you to have walked in with a smile and said "Julie, I have some **great** news!"*

I am so relieved that I am able to start my treatment that I leap out of the tiny cubicle and charge down the hall to the chemo room. A lovely nurse, Phyllis, introduces herself to George and me and says, "I don't think I ever met anyone so happy to get chemo before!"

"Where should I sit?"

"Any chair that's free."

I look around the room and see a large, open space where oversized, beige Lazy-Boy chairs are lined up in a circle facing the center of the room.

After I pick out my chair, I watch as Phyllis sets up my station. I am thinking about the movie Philadelphia, where Tom Hanks had AIDS and was hooked up to an IV bag, except I remember him having only one IV bag. My nurse hooks up at least five or six bags to my station. I ask what they are all for. She explains the tiny little bags are anti-nausea steroids and Benadryl to help me relax. Then there is this really large, bright, red bag. That's the "Red Devil," the one that makes your hair fall out. Then I have another large bag of clear liquid that is a different chemo "cocktail."

The nurse sprays my port to numb it while she connects my IV. The port is a small device that looks like a pace-maker. When they did my lymph node biopsy to see if the cancer had spread, they surgically implanted the port under my skin into my chest. That way they don't have to keep finding a vein and pricking me with needles every time I get chemo.

The chemo drip takes about five hours. I think I am handling it all very well until I realize that I am on page 46 of a magazine and haven't comprehended anything I've read. The magazine I have chosen is written completely in Spanish and I am not bilingual. I guess I am not handling this as well as I thought!

After another fifteen minutes or so, I start feeling really dizzy and weird, kind of light -headed and unable to focus. I become very anxious and irritated, almost to the point of hyperventilating. I call out to my nurse, "Help, help, " I am having some sort of reaction to the chemo! I don't think I can do this. Unhook me! Unhook me now!"

She calmly touches my hand and in the most soothing voice says, "Relax, Julie. Everything is okay. We haven't even started the chemo yet. You are just on the Benadryl drip right now and it will make you feel a little fuzzy."

*Great. Now I am known as the hypochondriac with cancer!*

# CHAPTER 4

## My Hair

**February 29, 2008**

At today's appointment Dr. Scary announces, "I have good news and bad news.

Your tumor is 98% estrogen- driven and it has a characteristic of HER2+ which is a more aggressive cancer. There is a drug called Herceptin that is designed to target this cancer. You will take this drug for one year after you are finished with your chemo, surgery and radiation."

I glaze over, but she continues anyway, "You will have four rounds of Adriamycin, a very strong chemotherapy, before your surgery. You have already had one dose of this, so you have three more to go. Hopefully those four doses will shrink the tumor enough to do a lumpectomy instead of a mastectomy."

She keeps on going, "After the surgery, you will have twelve more rounds of a different chemo called Taxol. You will then have radiation treatments every day for seven weeks, then you will begin the Herceptin, which will be administered through your port every month for one year. After all that is completed, you will take Arimidex for five years to block all excessive estrogen from your body."

"So...What's the good news?"

When George gets home from work, I realize we have to make some decisions as a couple. After today's appointment, I am starting to realize how extensive and time-consuming my treatments are going to be. I try to relay to him everything Dr. Scary had told me earlier, even though I was glazed-over through much of her monologue.

"Honey, that sounds like a lot to handle. Do you want me to go with you to your treatments?" George asks.

"I really appreciate the offer, but I know that taking that much time away from your business is not feasible. The truth is, you know I actually prefer going to my treatments alone anyway. I like talking to the other patients."

"I know baby, you are so independent." He wraps his arms around me in a big bear hug.

"Besides, one of us has to have a steady job right now!" I reply.

*I am learning that George and I approach trauma very differently.*

*I suppose my years in the corporate world in various management roles cause me to aggressively take charge and confront things head on, where he is more belabored in his approach. He tends to weigh his options and hope things will work out for the best. Since I find his approach uncomfortable, I instinctively know it is better for me and our relationship if I deal with a lot of the details of my care on my own.*

Receiving the overwhelming information from Dr. Scary today, on top of the excruciating pain I am in, makes tonight a particularly dark, low point. At 2 o'clock in the morning I am lying on top of my bed, soaked in a puddle of sweat. My hair has been falling out in clumps all day. As I run my hands through my scalp, it dissolves like cotton candy. I fill two small trash bags with hair and what remains is quite sparse. I am very nauseous and in agonizing joint pain from the Neupogen injection they gave me after my chemo treatment. The Neopogen keeps my white blood cell count up by pulling on my bones to make more bone marrow. At times, this is worse than the chemo side effects. The pain in my hips and legs lasts for hours.

I also am dealing with full body hot flashes that soak me, then leave me cold and chilled from being wringing wet. I had experienced hot flashes before and they were quite unpleasant but chemo elevates them to a whole new level. Not only do my neck and head feel like they're on fire, but my entire body goes through this cycle of feeling as if I am thrust into a furnace, drenched in my own sweat, then frozen from being soaking wet. I leave a trail of puddles in every chair and this cycle repeats at least twice an hour. Sometimes the flashes are relentless. I get them back to back. The only way to regulate my body temperature is to take a shower. This gives me a brief reprieve until the cycle begins again.

Lying on my bed, soaked in my own sweat, staring up at the ceiling, perhaps even at God, I mumble, "Okay, it's official, I've hit rock bottom." I numb myself with Xanax and doze off.

## March 1, 2009

Surprisingly, I wake up with no pain. George takes one look at me and gently whispers, "Honey, have you looked in the mirror this morning?"

When I catch my reflection, I gasp! I am horrified that George sees me looking so hideous. I wonder if I can have him hypnotized to forget the image that is now etched in his brain. I look like the Bride of Frankenstein, large patches of exposed scalp surrounded by long thin strands of hair.

*Being totally bald has got to look better than this!*

I call my hairdresser, Jane. She is amazing, "How about if you come to my house so we have some privacy?"

I carry a small shopping bag with my wig in it and George and I head to Jane's house. George babysits Jane's two small children while she and I go into her tiny bathroom to shave my head. I am pretty insistent about shaving it all off, but she does something wonderful for me. She knows I've never had short hair.

"How about if I give you a really short pixie? It will probably fall out in a couple of days, but at least you can see what you will look like when it starts to grow back in."

Jane cuts a cute short, short pixie following the shape of my head. I gaze in the bathroom mirror and think, "I don't hate this!"

But the true test is the expression on George's face. He could never play poker. He hates me to change anything about my appearance. Whenever I go for a haircut, he says, "Nothing too drastic, promise me!"

I slowly and shyly open the bathroom door to find George surrounded by Jane's kids. Toys are scattered all over the floor. My eyes lock with his as his expression softens and his face fills with love.

"Julie, who would have thought you would look this good with such short hair! I really, really like it."

I melt.

### March 4, 2008

We have a few days to enjoy the pixie, then that style starts looking really sparse. Plus, I am getting tired of drinking my hair as it falls into my coffee cup.

I want to see myself bald before anyone else does, so I lock myself in the bathroom and begin to shave my head with George's electric razor (*they make it look so easy in the movies*).

George hears the noise and asks, "What are you doing?"

"I am shaving my head. I don't want you to see me!"

He responds through the door, "Don't be ridiculous, let me help you. I love you."

I open the door and look up at him adoringly with the eyes of a small, scared child as he carefully and meticulously takes each section of my head and shaves it until it's smooth and shiny. This takes two hours. When he is done, we both look at my reflection in the mirror.

*I remember reading a book that said nothing quite prepares you for the sight of yourself bald for the first time.* For me, it is anti-climactic.

Every ounce of anxiety fades as George says, "Julie, you look absolutely beautiful."

No matter what bumps we face ahead as a couple, I will always remember this day and how full of love my heart is for him at this very moment.

# CHAPTER 5

## You Gotta Laugh!

**March 10, 2008**

My first really embarrassing side effect of chemo is a blister that pops up in an unmentionable area. I call my oncologist's office for advice.

"Hello, I need to speak with a chemo nurse."

"What is this regarding?"

"It's kind of personal." I mumble. *Great, I get the only male receptionist.*

"The nurses are all with patients. Can I take a message?"

I think to myself, *Julie, grow up. I am sure he's heard worse.* "I seem to have developed a blister from the chemo."

"Where?"

"It's kind of embarrassing." I burst out laughing as I realize there are other mortifying locations I had not thought of.

I am now forced to be quite graphic and specific as I ask to have a prescription called in to my pharmacy.

"Would you like the nurse to call you back to discuss this further?"

"Oh, God, No! I don't ever want to speak of this again!" We share a laugh just before hanging up.

A few hours later I go to pick up the prescription at the drug store. So now I have to make a judgment call. Do I pick up the embarrassing prescription and come back later for my other embarrassing purchases, or do I just bite the bullet while it's quiet and go for broke, getting everything all at once. Chemo wreaks havoc on your body and it's not sexy.

I look around the store and it's so empty you could literally bowl in the aisle. It's perfect timing for me to gather everything and get out of here without too much humiliation. I give the pharmacist my name and he informs me that I have three prescriptions waiting.

"Really? Three? What are they for?"

"Let's see, looks like this is for a rash or a blister of some kind. You've got one here for Compazine, which is a pretty strong anti-nausea drug, and this one is a steroid."

"They should just give us this stuff at chemo," I mumble. "I have to pick up a few more mortifying purchases…can I pay for everything here?"

"Sure." He smiles warmly. Somehow because he is wearing a clinical white lab coat and is old enough to be my father, I am not too embarrassed.

I search the store for the rest of my list, placing each item in my basket. Hemorrhoid cream—*check*. Nose bleed ointment—*check*. Heavy-duty laxative—*check*. Industrial-strength lubricant—*check*. Stool softener—*check*. Acne cream—*check*….Did I miss anything on my list? Yes, wig shampoo.

I run back through the hair product aisle looking for wig shampoo, feeling a frantic need to accomplish this before anyone sees me. When I can't find the shampoo, I bark at my new friend, the pharmacist, "You don't carry wig shampoo?"

He shakes his head no.

"Okay then, I think I am finally ready to check out."

Oh, no! There he is! Out of nowhere a really cute guy appears right behind me in line! Where did he even come from? I flush with embarrassment, which, of course, brings on a severe hot flash. I spontaneously throw a fashion magazine on top of the hemorrhoid cream. *God, please no! I pray nothing needs a price check!* Cute guy glances at all of my unappealing purchases and the only way I know to get out of this is to make a joke. Dripping relentlessly from my hot flash, I wink at him and say, "I bet you are so disappointed that I am already taken and you want to know if I have a twin sister?"

He smiles at me and winks back, "No thanks, I don't think I could handle all that!"

Later that evening, George comes home elated after a visit with his doctor. He is on a new medication for his high blood pressure. He is so excited that this new pill won't interfere with his sex drive. He is raring to go. Oh goody!

## March 15 , 2008

What would I do without these wonderful, hilarious dinners with my girlfriends! They are my lifeline.

One of my friends, who had gone through breast cancer treatments a few years earlier and had a lumpectomy, tells me, "If you are not symmetrical after your surgery, there are prosthetics that resemble chicken cutlets that you can put in your bra to make you look even on both sides." My sense of humor can't let this go!

One night, about ten of us went for dinner. My friend Sherry plays along, "Hey Julie, how about if I order my chicken parmesan with the sauce on the side so you can have the leftovers?"

"You are a true friend, Sherry!"

It becomes a long-standing joke that someone has to order chicken cutlets so I can take the leftovers home to stuff into my bra. None of us will ever look at chicken cutlets the same way again!

While we are all laughing about the chicken cutlets, I surprise everyone by pulling out "fake eyebrows" from my purse. A few weeks ago I had ordered them from a cancer catalogue. The picture promised "thick, lush, natural-looking eyebrows." What I received in the mail looked more like two dead caterpillars! I quickly pasted them onto my face where my eyebrows should be. We all laughed so hard we almost got kicked out of the restaurant! My friend Donna says, "You can dress up like Groucho Marx and wear them for Halloween."

There is comfort and lightness being with my friends and sharing my experiences. I know it doesn't matter to them what my hair looks like or if my breasts are real or uneven. I am still Julie and we can still laugh.

# CHAPTER 6

## Time to Reinvent Myself

**Sept 17, 2008**

I finally finished all of my chemo treatments! At the very end I had to switch to a different "cocktail" because my neuropathy was getting more severe and there is no way to tell if the nerve damage is reversible. I can't button my blouse or feel my hands and feet anymore, except if I have been standing or walking too long, then my feet burn like they are on fire.

A few weeks ago I started radiation treatments. I go every day for seven weeks.

My time slot is at 2:00 p.m. and I am so exhausted by that time that I have to drag myself out of bed to get there. I am starting to get very chafed and raw under my arm and breast area where the lumpectomy was. It is very uncomfortable and itchy.

Laura, the front desk coordinator at the radiation center, has become a good friend. She laughs at my jokes. Anyone who gets my humor is my instant friend.

Everyone I encounter at this center is wonderful. I can immediately tell that they see their work as a calling rather than a job. One time, when we were all gathered in a huddle, I teased, "Want to see how I give myself a haircut? I use a special technique, it's all in the wrist." I tug quickly at the back of my wig which pulls the bottom of the wig down and causes the bangs to instantly spring up. "Voila …I just trimmed my bangs!" We are all hysterical and I become known as the funniest patient they have ever had. Apparently the bar is set very low. I like these odds.

## October 20, 2008

Now that I am finished with the radiation, I am starting to think about my future. I still have to go to Dr. Scary's office every Friday for the Herceptin treatments. I am also having lower back and joint pain from the Arimidex. This is worrisome because I have to take this drug for five more years. I am so exhausted but I am ploughing through the cumulative effects of the last year.

When I feel well enough, George and I take half-hour ballroom dance lessons from our good friend, Tony. His beautiful ballroom studio transforms me and takes me to a world that has no illness and pain…only dreams and possibilities. Tony's exuberant energy motivates me to believe that I can reinvent my life. I feel I can soon put this past year behind me and start to move on with my goals and dreams.

Right before my breast cancer diagnosis, Tony and I worked together to design a dance/exercise class for women over fifty called Lady Fit.

*This is a far cry from my corporate career. It wasn't too long ago that I was entrenched in the politics and long hours of a high stress career in the telecommunications industry. When our office was relocating out-of-state and I was offered a severance package, I gladly accepted. I calculated from my severance that I had six months of savings to live on while I could figure out how to turn this new passion into a viable career path.*

To prepare for my new venture, I built up my credentials to teach the classes by getting a certification in weightlifting for women and a certification to teach Zumba Gold to the older population. I experimented with both morning and early-evening classes to see which times are the most successful. Just as my classes started to grow, I got breast cancer.

I can't keep up with all of the scheduled classes so I decide to keep teaching the most successful time slot, 9 a.m., every Monday, Wednesday, and Friday. Wednesdays are really fun because we all go out for breakfast after class. There's this great little cafe down the street from Tony's studio. It isn't a coincidence that Wednesdays are always our most popular class. It's a rule that you can't join us for breakfast if you don't exercise first!

Lady Fit is now growing and I have fifteen ladies that attend on a regular basis. They have been such an important part of my well-being through this past year. They didn't flinch when I first took off my wig and began teaching the class bald. The hot flashes were unbearable after exercising even a few minutes, so keeping a hot wig on my head was out of the question. Throughout the past year, they all came faithfully to class even when they knew I was often too weak to give them a motivating workout. When I am physically able, we go to the movies and dinners. We often joke, " We started out as an exercise group that would occasionally socialize and now we are a social group that occasionally exercises." I am finally beginning to heal—even if it is slowly. I have a vision for my future that I can really get excited about.

# CHAPTER 7

# It Runs in the Family

## November 9, 2008

George and I invite my mom and dad over to watch the mini-series, **John Adams**, on HBO. We become quite concerned about my dad. He doesn't look well and keeps dozing off on the couch during some of the most compelling parts of the show. I pull my mom into the kitchen.

"Mom, what's up with dad?"

"Oh, he has had this pain in his leg. You know you're father, he refuses to go to a doctor."

"I'm worried about him, Mom."

"Me too, Honey. I can't make him go, you know how stubborn he is. I agree with you though, I'll somehow make sure he gets it checked out."

About a week later I get a devastating phone call from my mother.

"Your father has bone cancer that has spread to his leg. They think it's lymphoma and can't find the origin of the cancer. He may need to have his leg amputated."

Every ounce of blood drains from my face. "Oh my God, Mom!" All I can manage to say is, "What's next?"

"He goes in for surgery to put a rod in his leg, but if they see that the cancer has already spread…." Neither my mother nor I can finish the sentence. "If the surgery is successful, the rod will be able to support his leg and he won't lose it."

### November 28, 2008

The waiting room at the hospital is so cold. Mom and I sit in silence, bundled in sweaters for hours, waiting to see if my dad's leg can be saved.

We try to wrap our fear in blankets to find some comfort. My father has never faced serious illness before. We know he will not survive emotionally if the rod can't save his leg.

After waiting for hours, the orthopedic surgeon finally appears. He is abrupt and as cold as the room. "Everything went well but we won't know for sure…," then he turns his back to walk out of the room without finishing the sentence.

I run up to him, my body blocking his so he can't leave. "Is my dad going to lose his leg? Is he going to be okay? Can't you tell us anything more?"

He takes a step back with an annoyed look on his face and barks, "I need you to calm down."

Oh no! He reminds me of Dr. Scary. I imagine them discussing me, *That daughter of his is so emotional, just tell her to calm down!*"

We wait another half-hour before we can see my dad. He is recovering in his hospital room. We don't even know if he's conscious yet.

My dad and I often speak in a language all our own, dropping cryptic hints that would seem odd to other people. We have discussed his deep convictions, and he has told me that if his mental or physical faculties were ever compromised, or he could not maintain a certain quality of life, he would want to die. So, we developed a code when he went into the hospital. If I ever want to truly know his state of mind, I ask him, "Hey Dad, who's your primary doctor?" If he answers with our code, "Dr. Kevorkian," I know he is still in there, with his sense of humor and mental faculties in tact.

Mom and I enter his hospital recovery room and find he's highly agitated and his body is violently shaking. I figure he is probably coming out of the anesthesia. I watch him for a long time, afraid to approach. When his shaking subsides, I ask our secret question, "Hey Dad…who's your primary doctor?"

He doesn't respond. His expression is foreign and distant.

I try again, but this time I lean closer, looking him in the eyes and grabbing his hand, "Dad, I need to know if you are okay. Who's your primary doctor?"

There's a brief twinkle in his eye. He squeezes my hand and softly whispers so only I can hear, "Dr. Kevorkian."

Relieved, I shout, "He's okay! Dad's okay!"

We soon find out that the surgery is a success and he will not lose his leg, but he'll need chemo. When I get home from the hospital that day, I feel enormous gratitude that the surgery was successful, but I am worried how my dad will handle chemo.

I can't sleep, haunted by the way his surgeon scolded me to "calm down." In the face of hearing terrifying news, why do doctors insist that I calm down?

As I think about my father's mortality, I find it ironic that how we handle illness will probably be one of the most profound experiences we share together. All of my life I have tried to connect more with him. He has been such a powerful and profound influence on me. I was always in awe of how much he knew about the world. We both read a lot, but I would forget details soon after reading them. Not my father.

I was amazed at how he knew so much about history and literature, not just to impress people at a cocktail party, but those textures of knowledge that separate true intellectuals from people with a good memory, nuances of detail that are only attained by truly loving to learn all there is to know about a subject.

He would frequently test me to make sure I was up on current events. Before getting together with my parents for dinner I would always make sure to read at least two newspapers cover to cover. He would subtly test me by throwing out a remote reference, expecting me to punt back. No topic was too obscure. Several years ago there was a recall on a certain brand of peanut butter. "Hey, Jul, you want a peanut butter sandwich?" This would be an innocent question to the untrained ear when it comes to bantering with Stanley, but his questions were always laced with an underlying test.

I quipped back, "How about if you eat one first and if you seem okay afterwards, I'll join you." We were both so pleased when I got the reference and I didn't have that dreaded "deer-in-the-headlights" expression.

Much of my love of learning comes from my father, that feeling of walking into a library or book store and being surrounded by all that knowledge, wanting to drink it all in. I treasured the rare moments when he really felt like talking about his life in detail. *Drop everything and listen…this is going to be interesting.*

Now, at home and well into his chemo treatments, I am waiting for him to be in the mood to talk. I ask, "Are you nauseous, Dad?"

"I just have no appetite." His frail, thin body is a shell of who he was just three months ago. When I look at my father from a certain angle, I barely recognize him.

Dad, you have to eat whether you feel like it or not. Can you still enjoy coffee?"

"You know up until my last chemo I could...now it tastes so metallic." I nod in agreement, remembering how much I missed enjoying a cup of coffee during my treatment. *It's not that you can't drink it...it just doesn't taste right.* "Do you still get the hiccups?"

"No... that's better."

"What about the numbing in your hands and feet?"

Out of all of the things I wanted to share with my father, who would have thought it would be our chemo side effects. Chemo didn't seem to destroy my frame, at least I was unaware if it did. I lost a few pounds but welcomed it. My father lost thirty pounds he couldn't afford to lose. His face is sunken in and the genetic dark circles he has always had under his eyes now seem to have taken over his face. He has no muscle tone and although I try to keep up with trimming his hair, it soon loses its shape because there's so little left.

Most heartbreaking of all is that he doesn't seem to read much anymore. My father, who defined himself by learning and reading, seems to be losing interest in life. He stares quietly for hours, not watching TV or listening to music, just wrapped in the chemo fog that I remember so vividly. I know from my experience that you can come out of this whole, but I am forty-seven years old and he is seventy-five.

# CHAPTER 8

# A Month of Anxiety

## January 5, 2009

A year has gone by since my diagnosis. I am still getting monthly Herceptin IV drips at Dr. Scary's office, but, thankfully, the harshest treatments are behind me. Even though I have not bounced back completely, I am optimistic about my future. I still have major problems with fatigue and joint pain, plus those relentless hot flashes have not subsided, but I am confident that, in time, these side effects will eventually fade.

Sooner than I expect it's time for my annual mammogram and sonogram. This will be the first test since my lumpectomy that will determine if I remain cancer-free. For me, the actual testing isn't the scary part, waiting for the results is what takes years off my life.

The mammogram goes fine, but during the sonogram I need a horse tranquilizer. I know the technicians who perform the tests are not allowed to relay specific information, but this particular sonogram tech is a bit sadistic with her initial questions. "You haven't had any follow-up testing for a year." she states with a judgmental tone. "How do they know the cancer is all gone?"

I am now frozen with fear and become mute. I know the technician has to be thorough in her test, but there is something so cruel about her utter silence as she keeps pressing the wand over and over the area where my cancer had been. I would feel so much better if she would just say something like, "Don't worry, I have to take a lot of pictures of the area where your surgery was to make sure everything's okay." But she says nothing. There is only the swishing sound of the sonogram wand and the repetition of her voice in my head, "*How do they know the cancer is all gone? How do they know the cancer is all gone?*" I have flashbacks to my last sonogram. I remember the tech putting stickers on the area where the lump was. I try to comfort myself. Maybe it's a good sign she isn't putting any stickers on me. When the test is over I feel a strange mix of relief and dread. Déjà vu. It's time to wait for the results.

### January 8, 2009

A few days have gone by since the mammogram and sonogram and I haven't heard anything. Just when I think I'm in the clear, my primary doctor's office calls. "Hello, Julie. You need to go for a cone magnification mammogram as soon as possible."

My life flashes before my eyes. I really thought I was done with all of this. I reply nervously. "I need to understand what this means!"

The young robotic voice on the phone sounds bored. "Let's see, (*I hear papers shuffling in the background*) the sonogram came back okay…but they want to take a closer look at the left breast. There is a cluster of calcifications that looks suspicious. You will need a special cone magnification mammogram." I think to myself, *I can't take this anymore, I need to be sedated NOW!*

## January 12, 2009

I zombie-out on Xanax. I think it's so funny when people say I'm so strong and have such a great attitude. I know I am not really handling any of it. Since my diagnosis, I have had unlimited access to Xanax.

Meanwhile, in total denial, I create an elaborate scenario to explain the mammogram results. I convince myself that the suspicious area must be the port. I don't remember if I told them that I still have a port in my chest from the chemo. *Yes, definitely, that must be what this is all about! It probably cast a shadow on the x -ray.* I am so sure of my theory that I tell the receptionist at the mammogram center, "I didn't mention that I had a port. I am sure that is the suspicious area you want to check. Can I go home now?"

The mute technician who did my sonogram is standing right behind the receptionist and all of a sudden she not only speaks, she has opinions. She coldly pipes in, "This has nothing to do with your port!" My stomach drops as she escorts me to a room with the slides from my mammogram hanging in plain sight. It's kind of weird seeing the silhouette of my breasts on the wall like an abstract art project. I try to butter her up to get some information. "You'll have to bear with me if I am freaking out. I went through an entire year of treatment and it's really scary that something else is going on. Can you show me exactly what the problem is?" I am begging and desperate for answers. She shows me three tiny white specs on the mammogram. They are little dots called calcifications. That's all she can tell me.

So, after the test I go home and do what every other 21st century hypochondriac would do. I google "calcifications on a mammogram." Apparently, if there are five or six calcifications in a cluster there is a high possibility that you're screwed, which begs the unanswered question…what about three dots?

## January 16, 2009

As I anxiously wait for my results, I spend the day with a friend and don't hear my cell phone ring in my purse. When I check the message, my primary doctor wants me to call him as soon as possible about the results of my mammogram. I am at least half-an-hour from home.

My cell phone plan only has sixty minutes for the entire month. I have spent hours on hold this month with various medical staff so I know my bill is going to be ridiculous but I am frantic and can't take the waiting any longer. I call my doctor right back.

"**Doctor's office, please hold.**"

*REALLY! Who answers the phone like that? Why answer the phone at all? You're cutting me off before you even know who I am or why I am calling?*

I remain on hold for the rest of the ride home. I won't be able to wait all weekend to find out what is going on. I'm coming undone. Meanwhile Verizon executives will be able to buy a summer home with the charges I incur for going so far over my allotted monthly minutes! Finally, when I'm almost home, the receptionist answers the phone and promises the doctor will call me that evening.

About 5:30 p.m. my primary doctor calls. He's calm, yet I realize he is concerned. "Julie, I looked at your report and there is a small cluster of calcifications that need to be biopsied."

"I don't understand. Why isn't the chemo working?"

"This may be a different type of cancer and they may need to change your treatment."

"Will I be able to have another lumpectomy or will I…?"

He interrupts me so I don't have to finish my thought,"Yes, this isn't like the other aggressive cancer you had."

"Well, it sounds like it's not the best news, but it's not the worst news either."

"Exactly." As we hang up I catch my breath.

## January 17, 2009

Another long wait at Dr. Scary's office. Finally, I am called in to see her.

"I have so much to talk to you about. What do these calcifications mean? Why isn't the chemo working?"

After taking my blood pressure, her first reaction is to angrily yell at me, "You need to calm down! You are going to have a stroke if you don't calm down!" Then, without waiting for me to respond to her caustic scolding, she tells me that a biopsy has to be done to determine if it is early stage or aggressive like the first tumor. She completely eliminates the possibility that it's benign. Then she does the most awful, insensitive thing...she matter-of-factly points to my breasts and says, "If it's invasive, they have got to go! You need to start considering a double mastectomy. Now I need you to calm down!"

I want to scream, *What the hell is wrong with you, lady?*

## January 18, 2009

Despite all of the anxiety-causing events of the past few days, I am doing surprisingly well. I have had a lot of talks with myself, *Julie...why are you hanging on for dear life to fifty- year old boobs...they're not what they used to be...for God's sake grow up!* I make jokes with my friends about having a "goodbye to Julie's boobs" party. This is the end of an era and it's time to say goodbye. I have evolved considerably from a year ago when I couldn't even say the "M" word. Now my new hobby is casually googling "nipple tattoos after a mastectomy."

## January 19, 2009

When I meet with my breast surgeon, Dr. Rodriguez, he is so much more understanding than Dr. Scary. The first thing he says to me is, "Julie, I totally understand why you would be a little freaked-out right now...I don't blame you one bit...you do understand this could be nothing?"

I respond in a very animated manner, "NO! No one has indicated this could be nothing!"

He visibly, yet subtly, shows his disgust with how I am being handled. I ask him questions about a double mastectomy and he puts up his hand to motion, "Stop, I do not want to discuss any of that until we get the results of the biopsy." He will have his staff set up the biopsy, but informs me that I need a referral from my primary doctor. My heart sinks as I know that getting a referral is not a simple request. Several Xanax-filled days are in my near future; trying to obtain a timely referral from my primary doctor's office is an ongoing nightmare.

## January 22, 2009

I call my primary doctor's office first thing this morning.

"Hi. This is Julie Klein. I need a referral for a biopsy as soon as possible."

The referral coordinator tells me, "Great news! I have it ready. You just need to pick it up."

I ask her, " When is the appointment?"

"Oh, you don't need an appointment, just come here first, then go across the street to the Medical Center and they will take you right away."

"Really?"

"Yes, the biopsy will be done right across the street."

"Perfect."

When I hang up the phone I think to myself, *this sounds too good to be true.*

The parking situation at the Medical Center is horrendous. I am forced to park about a block away in the "outpatient" area, which, considering my physical limitations, feels like miles.

I have walked about half-way to the entrance of the lobby. I am in agony. My back aches, my feet are on fire, I am miserable. I start to feel disoriented and light- headed. How am I going to remember where I parked? My shirt is soaking wet from the hot flashes. The walk completely exhausts me, but I enter the Outpatient Services smiling and waving the paper my primary office just gave me.

The receptionist looks up with one eye and says, "Can I help you?"

"I'm here for my biopsy."

"What kind of biopsy?" I show her the referral. "Oh… you need to go to building 2901 across the street."

I can't believe what I am hearing!

On the verge of tears, I stumble all the way back to my car, walking like I am ninety-years old.

I glance at the address and it looks familiar… *Oh My God! No!*

The biopsy location is actually in the same building as my primary doctor's office. I just spent the last hour using all of the strength I could muster trying to locate where to go for this damn biopsy and if the twelve-year old coordinator in my primary doctor's office knew her way out of a paper bag, she could have just said, "Julie…just go exactly one floor below my ass and you will be right there!"

I drag myself to the second floor of the building and see a large sign— "Women's Breast Center." I stumble to the reception area and say, "My primary doctor told me to come right over and get a biopsy today."

The woman behind the desk looks up at me through her glasses and sarcastically smirks, "Oh, really, now! They told you that you could just walk right in without an appointment and have a biopsy with no prep...Isn't that something."

*I feel my face flush with embarrassment. I should have known better. I should have trusted my gut, but I wanted to believe that something would go smoothly for once. Now I feel foolish and this woman is rubbing salt in the wound.*

I whisper, "Just tell me what I need to do."

She responds, "Your primary office needs to call and make an appointment for you."

*This sounds really stupid to me since I am already here...but I feel I have lost all credibility so I am forced to play along and follow her instructions.*

I just about crawl back to the third floor and inform my referral coordinator that she needs to call and make the appointment for me. She looks irritated, but picks up the phone. She quickly gets tired of waiting on hold and presses "1" to leave a message. I am not satisfied with this so I go back down one floor to the Women's Center and inform them, "My primary doctor's office is trying to call you to make an appointment and no one is picking up the phone...I want to make an appointment, please." The same sarcastic receptionist with the eyeglasses sliding down her nose says "Oh, you can't make an appointment through us."

"Why not? This is where I am coming for the biopsy?"

"You have to call **this** number." She hands me a piece of paper and says, "but their computers are down so you probably will not be able to get through."

"Can I just drive over there?" I am beginning to feel steroid rage coming on. Once my anger is triggered, I have no control over the rage from the steroids in my system.

"No…the scheduling center is in a remote location downtown."

Oh no! Now I feel my face flush with rage. Here it comes… "Steroid Julie" is triggered. I yell at the top of my lungs in the middle of the lobby, **"I am not looking for Dick Cheney in a bunker; I just want to make an appointment for a damn biopsy!"** I don't stop there. **"I know this doesn't mean anything to you, but the results of this biopsy are huge for me. It's the difference between 'You need a double mastectomy,' versus 'You are fine… you are cancer-free after a year of grueling treatment.' So please bear with me if I am losing it because you are telling me the only thing I can do to move this along is to call a number that won't be able to help me because their computers are down?"**

She casually replies, "Yep, that's pretty much the deal."
*Her indifference crushes my faith in humanity.*

When I get home and call the number, I am shocked that I get right through and easily make an appointment for Monday. However, I have to pick up all of my medical reports from the current mammogram and all of the reports from the first cancer, including these bulky, heavy, large films from my MRI that the medical profession refers to as "slides." I then have to deliver everything to the Women's Center before 5:00 p.m. today so the doctor will have time to review them before Monday's procedure. It is a little after 1:00 p.m., so I have a lot to do.

At the sickest and most harrowing time in my life, I am responsible for getting all of my prior records to the doctor before the biopsy can take place. I am then forced to drive all over town begging for my medical records from the many indifferent front desk medical staff who have no sense of urgency to help me. I have test results from my first cancer all over the county. I try to remember where I had all of my original tests done. There were so many: the mammogram/sonogram, MRI, PET scan, CT scan, and the biopsy pathology from last year.

I am so physically wiped out from the futile wild goose chase earlier in the day, believing I was getting the "walk in" biopsy, that I am tempted to hire a courier and a private detective to accomplish all of this by 5:00 p.m.

I buck up and realize that no one else is going to do this for me. Exhausted and weak, I forge ahead, functioning solely on adrenalin. One thing about "chemo fatigue," it is not like I can have a cup of coffee or take a nap and bounce back. Once I overdo it, my body completely stops functioning. I can't think to form words, my vision becomes distorted and the hot flashes become unbearable and relentless. Once I overdo it, I do not recover for several days and am forced to clear my calendar and recover in bed. I usually go to great lengths not to push myself beyond this point because I know the ramifications. However, today I am left with no choice and have to risk it.

There is a nanosecond when it occurs to me to take a deep breath and just reschedule the biopsy for later in the week, giving myself plenty of time to collect my medical records. However, every hour of not knowing my fate is so nerve-wracking to me, that I never seriously entertain the idea of postponing the biopsy. Plus, it took so much out of me just to get the damn appointment, there is no way I am rescheduling now!

After driving to four different hospitals, clinics, and "free-standing buildings," the last report I need to pick up is my biopsy from the first cancer. When I get to the medical records window, the hospital attendant tells me that it will take at least twenty-four to forty-eight hours to release the biopsy report. When I hear this, my legs buckle under me and I barely make it to the chair.

"Please, please, can you help me get those reports now? I am still going through cancer treatment and just found out I need a biopsy on the other breast. I can't take this anymore."

Her expression softens as she says, "Let me see what I can do."

I try so hard to express my gratitude but I am too weak to speak. I put my hand over my heart and mouth the words, "Thank You!"

I then drive frantically back over to the Women's Center for the third time today, hoping I make it before they close.

By the time I get there, at around 4:45 p.m., I feel like I have been standing on hot coals for hours. I pause for a moment before opening the door, remembering I had gone completely crazy and unleashed "Steroid Julie" just a few hours ago.

*They probably have a sign with my picture in the lobby, "Have you seen this woman? She is highly unstable and volatile!"*

My behavior earlier today is deeply troubling to me. This is not who I am...this is not who I will allow myself to become...I need to make it right.

Hunched over with my nose bleeding, I enter the center dripping blood and sweat all over the reports and slides. As I hand her the large, heavy pile of medical records, I try to smooth over the horrible impression that "Steroid Julie" made earlier in the day. I force a smile and announce, "Hello again! I'm really sorry about my outburst earlier. Can you believe that was me **on** Xanax?"

## January 28, 2009

I am not doing well. I had the biopsy two days ago and I'm jumping out of my skin with anxiety. Every time the phone rings I feel like I am going to throw-up because it could be the doctor calling with bad news. The physical and emotional ordeal of the biopsy has left me broken, frightened, and frail.

I am eyeing my closet to see if anything I own will get me through the time leading up to the double mastectomy and the plastic surgery for reconstruction. Even though my breast surgeon didn't want to discuss this possibility until the results came back, that is not how I handle bad news. I need to wrap my head around the worst-case scenario so I am prepared to cope, rather than being in denial and then falling to pieces when things don't turn out well.

As an agnostic and a pragmatist by nature, I cannot pray this away and believe everything will work out for the best. My questioning belief in a higher power makes the wait isolating and excruciating. I envy people who can turn their fear over to God and truly believe everything that happens is for the best and part of a master plan.

I do believe in **something**—a universal energy and even in the healing power of love, but that belief does not translate to prayer. In fact, if there is a God, what does that say about me if I only "hedge my bets" and feverishly pray when my life is in jeopardy? There is more integrity in being honest with myself. Why pray to something I am not sure really exits? Isn't that somewhat delusional?

I never discuss this with anyone unless I know for sure that we are on a similar page. Why on earth would I want to convince anyone to think like I do?

Recently, a long-time friend pressed me on the issue. I told her about my breast cancer and suddenly she had an urgency to visit me. We met at Starbucks and I had to endure a two-hour plea, "*Please, please* accept Jesus as your savior." The intention was sweet but very misguided. First, she miscalculated my silence all of these years which wasn't because I was still forming an opinion, but because I did not feel a necessity to convert her from believer to non-believer. Secondly, her urgency to convert me to Christianity did not bring me comfort as it reflected her assumption that I was going to die soon. The only way I knew to stop this unwanted exchange was to interrupt her and boldly declare my lack of faith.

She was dumbfounded.

"How do you cope with fear if you don't pray?"

"Xanax."

We both laughed.

It is one thing to face life as an agnostic before tragedy hits. It was easy to be brave during those invincible years when the death of a loved one or cancer were completely off my radar.

My first taste of what it really meant not to pray, or believe in a "better place" was in 1999 when my brother died suddenly. It was really the first time I had nothing to call upon to get me through tragedy...and it showed. I was thirty-seven years old and living under the illusion that I was a strong, independent, invincible woman who could take on the world. For one year after his death, I was so completely lost and ungrounded that I didn't know if I would ever feel lightness again.

People I knew would offer useless platitudes ... "He's in a better place" or "This was part of God's plan." None of these words provided any comfort for me, in fact, they made me feel more alone. This was the first time I really couldn't cope and had nowhere to turn for help.

The truth is, Xanax is my only course of action in moments of sheer terror.

Oh! That reminds me, I need to refill my prescription.

## January 29, 2009

It's not cancer!!!!!!!!

Around five pm, I get a call from my breast surgeon's office. "We just wanted to let you know that the results are benign."

"Really. Really! It's not cancer!"

"No, there is no cancer."

I turn into a blubbering idiot, crying into the phone, "Thank you so much…thank you… thank you! Give Dr. Rodriguez a hug for me! I love you… I love you!" Laughing and crying at the same time, I realize that giving them so much credit for the positive outcome is completely irrational, but I don't care. *Maybe this is going to be a good year after all.*

## January 30, 2009

This is the first day in a month I awaken without gasping in a cold sweat; my subconscious is no longer preparing me for a double mastectomy. It is the first morning I face the day without overwhelming dread and fear. Intellectually I realize I'm okay, but emotionally and physically the stress has taken a great toll on my already fatigued body and mind. Even in my relief I couldn't sleep, catatonically playing solitaire on my computer and drinking wine until 3:00 a.m., trying to calm my racing heart.

Throughout the entire month of January, I lived with the terror that there was cancer in my left breast while still being treated for cancer in my right breast. This is inhumane.

I know better care exists. I recently accompanied a friend who needed a breast biopsy. Her care was so superior to mine. She went to a wonderful doctor who did the sonogram right in her office, saw a suspicious spot, biopsied it right then and there and called her two days later, *on a Saturday*, to tell her the results. Her trauma of not knowing lasted three days.

I, on the other hand, with my HMO, had to wait almost as long for my biopsy results as the housekeeper, Mrs. Hughes, in **Downton Abbey** at the turn of the century…before telephone service!

# CHAPTER 9

# I wish I were Constipated

## April 16, 2009

I have a routine appointment with my gynecologist, Dr. King.

As he examines me he asks, "Have you been constipated?"

"No. Why?"

"We need to schedule an ultra-sound."

I panic, "What? Why? Do you feel something? Is it a mass?"

"I am 99 percent sure that it's nothing." *The last time I heard him say these exact words was when he felt the malignant lump in my breast, so I don't believe him.* I have this quirk in my personality of repeating myself when I am nervous. I begin to sound like Dustin Hoffman in **Rainman.** "Do you feel something? Is it a mass? Am I going to be okay? Do you feel something? Is it some kind of a mass?"

Then he says the worst thing he can say to me. "I need you to calm down. Nothing to be concerned about, but you may want to consider eventually having your ovaries removed as a precaution, since you had breast cancer." *Dr. King had performed a hysterectomy on me a few years ago, but left my ovaries so I wouldn't be thrown into early menopause.* He quickly dismisses me after the exam. "Glad you are doing so well after all your cancer treatments."

*Doing so well? Are you crazy?*

## May 13, 2009

Apparently I am not constipated. I endure an ultra-sound test that's so painful that I'm really scared that something is wrong.

## May 15, 2009

My primary doctor's receptionist calls, "You have a mass."

"What do you mean a mass? Is it cancer **again**? What kind of a mass?"

"That's all I can tell you."

In a panic, I call Dr. King's office and get his assistant, "They just told me I have a mass."

"Calm down Julie. Everything is okay. It's probably just a cyst. We are waiting for the results of your CA125 blood test."

"What's that?"

"That will determine if you have elevated blood levels for ovarian cancer."

"Ovarian cancer! Is that what you think this is?"

"No, we just have to rule it out."

I hang up the phone, reach for two doses of Xanax, then add more Pom Wonderful to my grocery list.

## May 16, 2009

My nerves are beyond shot! I am still not getting any definitive answers. This waiting is torture! I decide to have my ovaries removed either way. Dr. King's advice keeps running through my mind... *as a breast cancer survivor, it is often recommended to have your ovaries removed as a precaution.*

Even though my tests results are not back yet, I am terrified and I agree with Dr. King's advice to go ahead and schedule the surgery to remove my ovaries. He is very well respected in his field so I have no qualms about him doing the procedure.

## May 18, 2009
Finally! I get a call from Dr. King's office. My results came back from the CA125 test. I don't have ovarian cancer but my doctors are all in agreement that I should have my ovaries removed as scheduled. I am so relieved that it's just a cyst!

## May 20, 2009
Today is my outpatient procedure to remove my ovaries through my belly-button laparoscopically… *I can never pronounce this word.* I am also having my port removed while I am under the anesthesia. I am thrilled about this! It will be great to not have to look at this ugly bulge in my chest any longer! I am not really worried about the surgery as Dr. King assures me it is a very simple procedure. I feel confident that it's not cancer because of the blood tests results. I don't bring anything with me because I am going right home after the procedure.

The next thing I remember, I am lying on an icy cold, metal gurney in the operating room. I am shaking, vomiting, and freezing. There is a lot of chaos and commotion around me and I am struggling to wake-up from the anesthesia. Shivering uncontrollably, I ask for some warm blankets. I soon realize I am being brought to a hospital room and admitted.

When I become a little more lucid, I open my eyes and see George's worried, loving, blue eyes staring down at me. He is on one side of my bed holding my hand and my mom is on the other. The anesthesiologist enters my room and explains, " You had a mass wrapped from your ovary to your appendix. It looked like cancer, but it wasn't. A special surgeon was called in to take over this complicated procedure."

"No wonder I had trouble coming out of the anesthesia! How scary! I'm so relieved it's not cancer!"

## May 27 , 2009

I just got home from the hospital last night. This morning I have to go for my surgical follow-up appointment with Dr. King.

He's usually cold and distant, but today as I enter the room, he gives me a big bear hug and exclaims, "It's so great to see you!" Then he solemnly sits down and looks me in the eye. "Yeah, turns out we have got a bit of bad news—shocking really—turns out that you have cancer of the appendix. Dr. Rodriguez and I were shocked."

*Dr. Rodriguez is shocked? What about me?* Horrified, I reply, "What? I don't understand? How can this be? Will I need **more** chemo? I just finished the chemo from the breast cancer."

"You may need another surgery, but I think we got it all, do you understand me? You're okay. Are you understanding what I am telling you? Six months from now… whew…you would have been in big trouble. Oh, by the way, you still have one ovary. I'm just a gynecologist, I couldn't do the surgery, but you are okay. Do you understand?"

*This nervous pattern of repetitive speech is familiar to me, but I have never heard it from a **doctor** before. Who sounds like **Rainman** now?*

I get in my car and head straight to my parent's house. I am in shock, yet lucid enough to worry about how I am going to break this news to them. I don't bother knocking on their front door, I just barge in. My mother sees my face and asks, "What's wrong, Honey?

"I've just come from my appointment with Dr. King. They got it all, but apparently they removed a cancer in my appendix."

"Julie. I knew something was very wrong! I saw Dr. King's pale face when he came out of the surgery. That …man… was…**scared**!"

## May 31, 2009

Sunday evening around 10:00 pm the phone rings. George and I are surprised to hear it's my breast surgeon, Dr. Rodriguez. The tone of his voice is serious. He has always been the clear, calm, level-headed voice of reason that I turned to when Dr. Scary terrified me. So, at first, I am relieved to have an update from him instead of her. He bluntly informs me, "You have a type of cancer called mucinous adenocarcinoma of the appendix. This cancer is the 'real deal.' You will need to have another port put in and have six more months of a different kind of chemo than you had for your breast cancer." When enough silence passes for him to assume I heard and digested all of that, he solemnly adds, "And you need to have another surgery to remove a third of your colon. The wrong surgery was done on you."

I am much too shocked to speak.

He explains that the nature of this cancer is very difficult to treat once it spreads. "There are mucinous or mucous-like cells that jump through the digestive tract and form more cancerous tumors. The only way to treat this is to have a life of constant 'debulking' surgeries to continually keep removing all of the tumors. There are experts in this type of surgery, but none of them are local. I need you to come to my office tomorrow to discuss your options."

"Will I need a colostomy bag?" *If the answer is yes, I'm done. I know I can't handle this.*

"No. Hopefully the surgery can be done laparoscopically with minimal recovery time."

I hang up the phone and feel all the blood drain from my face. I am violently shaking. George asks me if I am cold as he wraps a blanket around me.

I whisper in his arms, "No, I am terrified."

## June 10, 2009

I quickly learn how rare and difficult it is to treat this cancer. Dr. Rodriguez is now my primary source of guidance. Even though Dr. King was in the operating room, he clearly has expressed that the situation is beyond his scope of expertise. I don't know why my oncologist remains out of the picture, as logic would dictate she should be calling the shots, but I dislike her bedside manner so much that I don't initiate contact. Her lack of initiation and involvement is puzzling. I feel both relieved and abandoned by it.

When I get to Dr. Rodriguez's office for the consultation, instead of waiting in a cubicle like I always had in the past, he escorts me to his private office. He is stammering and uneasy as he reiterates what he told me over the phone, but now he is pondering if I have some sort of auto-immune disease. I have never seen him so unsteady. I am baffled by his behavior. He was my rock during the first cancer, so the contrast is very unsettling. He adamantly attempts to persuade me to go out of my HMO network and call a world-renowned specialist in treating cancer of the appendix. He expresses that no one locally is qualified to do this type of surgery. When I show concern about my insurance not covering out-of-state doctors, he replies, "Don't you want the best care you can find?" I feel completely overwhelmed and ill-equipped to make this decision, plus there's something uncomfortable about him pressuring me not to consult with any local colon surgeons. He must sense my hopelessness because what he suggests next completely blows my mind!

**"How about if I learn how to do the surgery myself, with the virtual guidance of the out-of-state specialist."** I am left speechless by his offer. I agree to call the world-renowned specialist to see if they can somehow work with my insurance company.

"I appreciate your offer." I reply. "Let me call you after I talk to them."

Once home, I make the phone call. I explain to the woman answering the phone that I am calling from out-of-state and I would like to make an appointment for a consultation. She abruptly tells me that this doctor is far too busy to do consultations. She then asks for my diagnosis, after which she recites the following words that I am sure will haunt me for the rest of my life. "Your insurance will not pay for the treatment you need. When you decide you are ready to save your life, bring $30,000.00 to our facility and we will schedule your procedure. When you are serious about your survival, you call us to schedule the surgery. This kind of cancer always comes back. If you do not get treated with us, your life will consist of one surgery after another to keep removing all of the tumors until you eventually succumb to your disease within two to four years."

With no transition to allow me to digest what she has just told me, she asks if I'm ready to battle my insurance company to get them to pay a small portion of the cost. She never explains why he is the only doctor who can effectively treat this cancer.

Emotions swirl in my head… terror, confusion, anger. I don't know who to trust. Could my life be in immediate jeopardy? Am I dying? Was the person I just talked to a doctor or a receptionist? She never explained more about this procedure! She never asked me if my cancer had spread! This is just too much to bear…where is my Xanax?

### June 12, 2009

I am shaken to the core from that phone call... *that "world-renowned" expert's office hasn't even seen my medical records! How can she give me a death sentence over the phone when she hasn't even seen my pathology or read my case? Something isn't right about Dr. Rodriguez's role in all of this. Why on earth would a breast surgeon offer to learn an extremely intricate virtual colon surgery? Why would I agree that this is the best option without talking to local colon surgeons? I am feeling completely alone, confused and abandoned by the medical profession. How do I contend with a diagnosis that I don't understand, plus the behavior of my doctor is absolutely unbelievable and jolting.*

Today will reveal my fate... I have a PET scan scheduled to determine just how bad this situation is. If the cancer has spread, I am in real trouble. So, once again, I wait for results of a test that will dictate the quality and/or duration of my life.

The young woman who coordinates my appointments and tests in my primary doctor's office is witnessing first hand what I am enduring. She is one of the people I sarcastically had been referring to as the " twelve-year old." She is now showing concern and becoming very involved in my care. She is also quite anxious to find out the results of my PET scan and promises she will have the doctor call as soon as the results are back.

### June 14, 2009

My new friend calls, "Julie, don't call the out-of-town specialist just yet—we have your PET scan results."

"Is it bad news?" I plead.

She calmly says with a laugh in her voice, "You know I can't discuss anything with you...the doctor has to give you the results."

For a moment I am confused, forgetting that she cares about me. "You know what I have been through, you have to give me a clue, please!"

"Julie, listen to my voice. Do I sound happy?"

Startled, I take a deep breath. "Yes, you do."

"Well, I am happy for a reason."

"OH MY GOD, I am clean, everything is okay on the PET scan!" We are both giddy. "You didn't hear it from me. The doctor will be calling you soon."

At that moment, a warmth comes over me for my friend. I hear the love and joy in her voice. She's truly, genuinely happy. From this day on, I only use her name and never refer to her as "the twelve-year old" again. Her beautiful name is Arianna.

*This moment is significant for me. Throughout my journey, I felt my life was worth saving; however, I encountered so many people who blatantly did not care if I lived or died. It was so difficult dealing with these individuals, yet I needed them for my survival. They are the people who get my referrals, schedule my tests, or coordinate my surgeries. One of my greatest challenges is learning to communicate without anger and with full knowledge that I am nothing to many of them. I continually feel so alone in the quest to save my life without losing my sanity or my sense of kindness. To remain kind while facing injustice takes a remarkable amount of self-control.*

*For the first time, I am no longer invisible to Arianna. There's someone in the medical bureaucracy who actually sees me. I had become her friend, Julie, and she cares whether or not I live.*

My primary doctor calls me on my cell phone while I am sitting in Dr. King's lobby waiting for my second follow-up appointment since my surgery.

"Julie, I have the results of your PET scan. There is no evidence of cancer anywhere…breast, liver, colon…around the area of the excision…nowhere."

I cry out with joy, not caring who in the waiting room hears. "Really? I am *really* cancer-free?" About five strangers in the waiting room applaud. If I were in a bar, I would buy a round of drinks for them, instead I say, "Everyone's co-payments are on me!" I am so thrilled that this nightmare is really over. I keep smiling and repeating to myself, *"I am cancer-free. I am cancer-free! Life is beautiful."*

After all of the conflicting information I have had to recently sift through, I now believe that the best course of action is to do nothing. I am cancer-free…I don't know what to think of my breast surgeon's offer, not to mention what was said to me by the world renowned specialist's office. As far as I'm concerned, I am going to focus on being cancer-free and tell them all to "Go to Hell!"

### June 19, 2009

Still on a bit of a high from the wonderful news, I drive to my very last breast cancer Herceptin treatment! I do not have an appointment with Dr. Scary, since I don't actually see my oncologist every time I have treatment. Usually it's about every third visit. I am so relieved I don't have to interact with her today. I can just get through my last cancer treatment in peace! I reflect upon my relationship with Dr. Scary and how it went sour.

*To be fair, I must clarify that her diagnostic ability is excellent and I do vaguely recall having a brief consultation with her about the second cancer. I remember being dismissive and telling her I was probably going to seek treatment out-of-state. I just told her that so I didn't have to endure her terrifying take on the situation, followed by her inevitable scolding to "calm down." Her bedside manner and sharp insensitivity are intolerable. She proclaims worst-case scenario outcomes before she has all the evidence to support her* blunt assessment. Her demeanor is scattered and rushed and she mumbles as if she were talking to herself, making me feel as though my presence in the room is irrelevant. There's definitely a mutual dislike. I mull over various explanations to justify her dislike of me, because it couldn't possibly be my charming personality. I survey everyone in the lobby to see if my opinion is shared by her other patients. I have plenty of time to do my informal interviews because she makes her patients wait in the lobby at least two hours for every appointment. Then we wait in an icy-cold, claustrophobic private exam room, wearing a thin, paper vest for about another half-hour. The cold temperature is a plus for me because of my hot flashes, but I imagine it is quite uncomfortable for other patients. As she approaches the closed door of the exam room, I hear the sound of her intimidating heavy heels clicking in the hallway, warning me that she's about to enter.

When interviewing the other patients, I do not let on that I don't like her. I innocently ask, "So how is it going with Dr. Scary?" I hear reviews like:

"I know the wait is long, but she is totally worth it."

"She cares so much and takes her time with every patient."

"She is just so wonderful."

Okay, So, it's me. She doesn't like **me**. Everybody likes me! In my whole life there have been maybe two or three people EVER who didn't like me. Of all of the people on the planet who don't like me, isn't it ironic that the person in charge of saving my life is one of them?

There must be a reason for this as I reflect on my prior meetings with her. When she says something that terrifies me, I immediately run like a little tattletale to my breast surgeon, Dr. Rodriguez, for clarity and soothing. I have done this many times now and I am sure he then scolds Dr. Scary. I don't do it out of disrespect, but for my own emotional survival.

*I remember when I first met her. I opted to have four rounds of chemo first before my lumpectomy to shrink the tumor. By doing this, the tumor would be so small that the surgery would be easier and cosmetically more pleasing. So, after the fourth chemo, when I could barely feel the tumor, I asked the logical question,"Doctor, how much of my breast will be removed since the tumor is now so small?"*

*"Oh, about a quarter," she responded cavalierly.*

*"What!" I exclaimed. "If I had known that up front, I would have opted for the mastectomy!" She offered no comfort or explanation, just shrugged her shoulders.*

*I went home and positioned my hand to remove a quarter of my breast. Great! I am going to look like a mismatched freak! A double D and a triple A! After losing a week of sleep, I called Dr. Rodriguez for comfort.*

*"Julie, it's not like slicing a cake that will leave a gaping hole. I promise you that I am really good at what I do, and I will make you look as symmetrical as I can."*

*I am still shaken, imagining stuffing my bra with a chicken cutlet every day to look more symmetrical. "Can I have a plastic surgeon fix me if I look weird?"*

*"I am confident you won't need one. I am so sorry she scared you unnecessarily. This is **my** area of expertise, not hers."*

*Shortly after that she definitely began to distrust me. She even made a comment to me once, "Now don't go running to Doctor Rodriguez about this." That was the last question I ever asked her. If I thought of questions, I would save them for Dr. Rodriguez, or even research them myself. Can you believe that medically trolling the internet for answers is actually more soothing than talking to my oncologist?*

As I pull into the parking lot of her office, I realize I can't change what has transpired between us. I am still feeling abandoned by her notable absence about this second cancer; it's still so odd to me that she is allowing Dr. Rodriguez to completely take the lead on this. As I go up in the elevator, I feel a wave of anxiety as I open the door. The familiar chemical smell hits me as I head back to the chemo room.

I pick out my Lazy-Boy Chair and begin to prepare for my very last treatment. It is slowly sinking in that after today I am finally done with cancer. A lightness washes over me and I remind myself that in just a few hours, I am free.

One of my favorite chemo nurses sits down next to me, which is highly unusual. They are all wonderful but are probably trained to keep their distance emotionally.

"Julie... how are you doing?"

"Great! I just got a clean PET scan!"

"You do know you need more chemo."

"No, I have a clean PET scan." *I am wondering why she has my records in her hand.*

"Julie, your cancer spread to the outer tissue. You need another surgery and six months of chemo for colon cancer."

"What? Why? I don't understand."

"Julie, you are an intelligent person. Why wouldn't you take this precaution?"

I want to scream,*"Because more surgery and more chemo will kill me!"* but I say nothing.

She then relays in great detail what is in store for me. "The port goes back in on the other side to prepare you for more chemo. After the surgery to remove part of your colon, you will immediately begin six months of colon cancer treatment. You will have a fanny pack that holds the chemo in it and you will wear it for three days in a row, then you will be off for two weeks, then resume three days on again/off again for six months. The three days you are on the chemo will be constant 24/ 7."

She hands me the scariest printout I have ever seen, including a pie chart/graph that explains I will die in five years without chemo. After she finishes her explanation, I ask to see the fanny pack. I need to see what I may be facing, I can't fathom being attached to my chemo. I need to know what this contraption looks like. She must have forgotten my request and gone to lunch because she never returns.

Devastated, I sit in silence getting my Herceptin treatment, trying to digest everything I have just heard. I am emotionally broken, utterly broken beyond repair. Here I was lightheartedly thinking this was my last treatment, and then I hear that I will have to start all over again...actually attached to chemo for three days at a time!

I am too upset to notice my surroundings. A young woman, probably around thirty years old, is next to me. She notices I am visibly devastated and withdrawn. She jars me by leaning over and whispering something in my ear. "You know, from what I have read about battling cancer, attitude is everything."

Rage surges through my body. I realize she is with an older woman, probably her mother, who's getting treatment. This idiot doesn't even have cancer and she is giving me advice about my attitude!

"You don't know what you are talking about. I was the poster child for having a great attitude during the first cancer and what good did it do me? I can **definitely** tell you that attitude is **not** everything." I turn my body so my back is now facing her.

I call over one of the other nurses, "Patty, come here a minute, I need to ask you something."

"Julie, what is it? What's wrong? You are not your bubbly self...isn't today your last Herceptin treatment?"

I explain to Patty in great detail what the other nurse had told me and ask if I can see what a fanny pack looks like. I meekly whisper, "It sounds inconceivably awful to be attached to my chemo for three days at a time, nonstop." I show her the printout I was just given, the pie chart mapping out my poor life expectancy, both with and without chemo.

Her face goes white. "Have you discussed any of this with the doctor?"

"Nope! This is all shockingly new to me." She suddenly looks just as frightened as I am.

When my Herceptin treatment is over, I am so shaken and upset that I dent the front of my car on the way out of the parking lot. I am now recalling Dr. Rodriguez's chilling Sunday night phone call a few weeks ago and realize that what the nurse just told me supports his assessment that this is a scary cancer and it is not to be taken lightly. This is so devastating... I really thought that after the clean PET scan, he was just over-reacting. I can't just brush this off now, but why did I hear this from a nurse and not Dr. Scary?

While I am still in my car, my cell phone rings. Patty, the nurse who showed me the fanny pack is calling. "Julie, I... uh...I just want to make sure you are okay. You seemed really shaken up when you left the office. I don't want you to think we were giving you definite details about your treatment plan...that can only come from the doctor. Are you okay? We hope we didn't upset you."

"Hi Patty, Yes, of course I am upset, but I do really appreciate you being honest and explaining everything to me."

"Just make sure you talk to your oncologist about all of this."

*As I hang up my cell phone, I see Dr. Scary's office in my rear view mirror and have the strong feeling that no matter how this unfolds, I won't be coming back to this office ever again.*

I don't consciously plan on it, but I drive to my parents' house, looking for someone I love and trust to guide me through this terrifying maze.

I walk in the door and my mom leaps out of her chair to hug me.

"Hi Honey, I didn't expect to see you today."

My father is in a catatonic post chemo fog. His emotional recovery has not gone well. He has refused to go to a rehab facility where they would help him learn to walk with the rod in his leg. As a result, he's having trouble adapting to the walker. It takes him a long time to rise up out of a sitting position and navigate the walker without falling.

He doesn't seem to be engaged in anything going on around him and I don't even know if he realizes that I've entered their house until I explain what happened at Dr. Scary's office. I show my parents the pie chart of my projected dire life expectancy, both with and without chemo. I explain how the nurse was adamant that I should follow the protocol of six months more chemo for my best chance of survival. My mom shoots many logical questions at me, too quickly for me to address each one:

"Why didn't this come from Dr. Scary instead of the nurse?"

"Why would they show you such a terrible chart?"

"I don't understand, your PET scan is clear?"

"Why do you need more chemo?"

"You need another surgery? I don't understand?"

"You just had the port removed, now they want to put it back in again?"

In the midst of my mother's questions, my father slowly rises from the couch with his arms struggling to hold himself up on his walker. His face is distorted and angry. He stands up as straight as his frail body will allow and screams at the top of his lungs, "JULIE, I FORBID IT! I ABSOLUTELY FORBID YOU TO GET MORE CHEMO!" His whole body is shaking.

This stops me in my tracks, standing motionless as I face him. In my entire life, I cannot recall my father ever uttering the words, "I forbid it" to me. In fact, he has never screamed at me, ...ever.

I understand in this moment that my father doesn't want to accept that I may have to suffer even more. He knows first hand what chemo is like. He's finishing his sixth round and it's breaking him. He knows I have already had twenty rounds of toxicity, and he feels six more months of relentless poison seeping through my veins will forever change my life in ways neither of us can predict. He knows that my body desperately needs time to heal from the first cancer.

After a lot of emotional ranting from all three of us, I ask my father if he's comfortable if I go to his oncologist for a second opinion. My father calms down and nods his head. "Yes, I trust Dr. Roman."

Devastated by my news, my father does not speak or eat for several days afterward.

# CHAPTER 10

# My Hero!

**June 22, 2009**

That following Monday morning, I go without an appointment to my primary doctor's office to see if I can get a referral to Dr. Roman.

On an HMO, all of my care is coordinated through my primary doctor. That office is responsible for all of the approvals and referrals from my insurance company. I can't get approved for a second opinion or make any healthcare decisions without first consulting and waiting for approval from my primary doctor if I expect my insurance company to pay for anything.

As I walk in the door, I see my new friend, Arianna, behind the desk.

" Arianna, you'll never believe what's going on… even though I got a clean PET scan, my doctors are still recommending more chemo and surgery."

"Oh, Julie, I thought you were done with all of that when you got the clean scan. I'm so sorry!"

"Can you squeeze me in to see the doctor today?"

"Of course! We are all concerned about you! I know he will want an update."

I am now in the awkward position of clearly explaining what has transpired to my primary doctor so he can determine what I should do next. I think about the irony of it all:

*I knew early on that a medical career was off the table for me, as I have been very squeamish my entire life. I passed out cold dissecting an earthworm in high school. One whiff of the formaldehyde, coupled with the thought of cutting into something with organs, was too much for my delicate system to bear. I even get woozy and have to shield my eyes when watching a mildly bloody episode of CSI. How ironic that the terms mucinous adenocarcinoma, peritoneal cavity, and right hemi-colectomy are now just everyday words in my vocabulary.*

I am quickly taken back to a cubicle and my primary doctor walks in.

"Hi, Doctor, well, our good news about the PET scan was short-lived. Apparently my other doctors think I am not out of the woods despite the clean PET scan. My breast surgeon thinks that I need to have one third of my colon removed, a right hemi-colectomy, to ensure that any cancer cells that escaped during the first surgery won't spread. He strongly feels that I need to go to a specialist in Washington, D.C. This would require cashing in my retirement to pay $30,000 for a very specialized procedure called a Hot Chemo Wash. The financial hit would be devastating but what good is a 401K if I am dead?"

I take a deep breath and continue: "Here's how the Hot Chemo works…the expert surgeon places hot chemo directly into the peritoneal cavity, the area in the stomach where the cancer originated, basically boiling my organs to rid them of cancer cells. Although statistically proven to be highly effective at killing the cancer, it is a very aggressive treatment that may kill me too."

My primary doctor's mouth falls open as he listens to me.

"My oncologist, whom I have absolutely no relationship with any longer, thinks this can be treated by surgery and conventional chemo." I relay to him the incident at Dr. Scary's office when the chemo nurse explained the fanny pack and the six months of being attached to the chemo via an IV.

He nods his head as he begins to understand why further treatment may be necessary, but I can tell by his face that he's uncomfortable with how I'm being tossed around like a ping-pong ball. "Have you considered a new oncologist for a second opinion?"

"Funny you should ask! I love my father's oncologist, is there any chance he takes my insurance?"

My primary doctor again nods and smiles when I mention Dr. Roman. "I know Dr. Roman, he is a top-notch oncologist and he takes your insurance. I am confident you will be in good hands."

## July 1, 2009

I meet with Dr. Roman. My first pleasant surprise is that I don't have to sit nervously in the waiting room for two hours. Instead, I am escorted to a private cubicle within fifteen minutes. As I walk through the office, it resembles Dr. Scary's, but I notice there's no weird chemical smell. I peek into the chemo room and see the familiar La-Z-Boy chairs in a semi-circle attached to IV poles. It's eerily similar to the room where I had gotten my breast cancer treatments. A wave of nausea sweeps over me when I think I may have to spend even more time reclining in one of those ugly, beige, leather chairs.

As Dr. Roman enters the room, I am struck by how handsome he is. This is actually a deterrent for me. The last thing I need now is to get flustered or shy around him. I need to have a clear mind. I can't be worried about trivial bullshit, *I wonder if he thinks I'm pretty? For God's sake Julie, wake up, you are a bald, middle-aged woman whose body keeps growing aggressive, cancerous tumors. The only thing intriguing about you is that you are still alive. He's not going to find you attractive. On the other hand, compared to the rest of the pasty skeletons disintegrating in the waiting room...*

I recall my father's description of him,

"*I am lying in my hospital bed and in walks this tall handsome guy who looks like Omar Sharif, 'Hi, Stanley, I'm your oncologist.*"

There is a marked difference between Dr. Roman and Dr. Scary. He's calm and prepared. Unlike Dr. Scary, she enters the room in a fluster, with papers flying all over the place. She has to reacquaint herself with my case every time I meet with her.

At first, I am skeptical and cautious in my demeanor with him. After the last few months, I don't know if I can trust anyone in the medical profession anymore.

He begins with the question, "So tell me why you are considering switching doctors?"

I want to make a good first impression so I don't appear to be the cause of the "personality conflict" with Dr. Scary. For this reason I hold back and try not to allow "Rainman Julie" or even worse, "Steroid Julie " to escape. I'm so afraid I'll sing like a canary, revealing my true feelings about her. Any minute I can lose control of my tongue and verbally launch into a childish rampage, laced with extensive caustic profanity. "*I fucking hate her, she is the most insensitive, alarming, over-reactive bitch! You have no idea how many times she has unnecessarily scared the crap out of me. Who the hell says 'the results of your biopsy are auspicious?*"

"We just didn't click." I reply.

His intuitive grin reveals he knows there is much more to the story. Then he perceptively asks, "I was reviewing your case last night and it appears as though I am missing four months of your file. I see that you found the lump yourself in October, 2007, but I don't see anything in your file until mid-February, 2008?"

"Nope. You have the entire file." *I feel giddy… I love where this is going!*

He scrunches his face in puzzlement and horror, requiring me to elaborate as he studies my reaction.

I can't control my emotions anymore and I blurt out, "My HMO wants me to die!" *So much for making a good impression.* "My insurance company kept finding reasons to delay or deny most of my appointments and treatments."

"What?" he pleads for me to continue.

"I would make an appointment for a test or consultation, then the day before I was supposed to go I would get a call with some lame excuse as to why I couldn't go to a certain doctor or facility. Then, to top it all off, I couldn't find a local oncologist who accepted my insurance. The idiot at my HMO kept insisting that the closest one was two hours away. I knew this couldn't be true, we live in the retirement capital of the world. I couldn't get anyone to listen to me! I spent a week getting transferred from one incompetent twelve-year old office worker to the next. It turns out that my HMO classifies oncologists under "H" for Hematology/Oncology. I found it incomprehensible that my HMO staff did not know this! **Could it be possible that I am the first person who ever survived the HMO nightmare maze long enough to even need an oncologist**! Anyway, before I know it, it's February and I still have this damn tumor growing inside of me! Do you know that my HMO will not approve any test that is done at a facility that is attached to a hospital or medical facility because it is more expensive? So, while my tumor cells are rapidly reproducing, I am wasting precious time calling clinic after clinic, trying to find a facility that my insurance will approve. Do you realize how crazy I must have sounded, 'Hello, is your facility a free-standing building or are you attached to a hospital? You are attached, okay, thank you for your time. Do you know of any places that are not in any way attached to clinics or hospitals that do this test?' When I finally found a clinic that my insurance approved, a week after I took this test called a Muga scan, to see if my heart is strong enough to withstand the chemo, they call me back and tell me the machine was broken that day and I have to retake the test. Get this, I had to have this highly radioactive substance intravenously shot into my blood stream, then I had to wait for about a half-hour before they took images of my heart. While I was waiting for this toxic substance to travel through my body, I was kept in a separate room because I was, apparently, too radioactive to be around other humans. Dr. Roman, you can imagine how I felt having to take this dangerous test twice in one week? They had tried to console me by explaining this second test was 'on the house' since it was the facility's fault that the equipment malfunctioned. The good news is that I will never get hit by a car walking at night because now I glow in the dark."

He stares at me in disbelief. "So let me get this straight, you have stage three aggressive cancer and your care is delayed for four months because of bullshit red tape?"

*He gets it! He really gets it!*

In this very instant my world becomes so much lighter. I am too overcome with emotion to speak, so I vehemently nod my head, indicating not only my appreciation of his understanding of the situation, but also his appropriate expression of disgust. I also love that he curses when he is outraged.

With tears now uncontrollably streaming down my face, I ask, "Dr. Roman, I would be so grateful if you are not just a second opinion. Could you please be my oncologist and take over my care?"

Nodding, as if he already has assumed this role, he eagerly explains his thoughts on my treatment. "I am starting from scratch and not necessarily agreeing with your diagnosis. It is more statistically likely that your breast cancer spread to your ovaries and this is not a new cancer. The odds of a new primary tumor are very unlikely. I am having my lab evaluate your pathology. I know you want answers, but bear with me, I need to get this right. Until I know what type of cancer it is, I am not going to discuss any treatment yet. Just know I will not advise more chemo or surgery unless it is absolutely necessary... you have been through enough! I want you to have the genetic BRCA1 and BRCA2 tests to see if you test positive for the breast cancer gene. Your Ashkenazi Jewish heritage puts you at a higher risk. The results of that test will influence how we proceed."

"I wanted to do that test before but my insurance won't..." He interrupts me, takes my hand and leads me down the hall. He sits me in a chair and instructs the nurse, "I want a BRCA 1 and 2 on her STAT."

I feel more tears of gratitude well up in my throat. "Doctor... .I don't think my insurance will cover..."

"You leave that to me."

I absolutely love this man. I am humbled by his complete ownership of my survival. He is my hero and boy do I need one!

## July 9, 2009

Today I have my second meeting with Dr. Roman. He confirms that the pathology definitely is cancer of the appendix. To our surprise, it looks like my original team of doctors was correct.

I do not fault him for doubting the original diagnosis. To the contrary, I so appreciate his thoroughness in assuring that we have the correct diagnosis.

Now that he has confirmed the diagnosis, I update him on what has already transpired with my other doctors. "Dr. Rodriguez believes that the only way to effectively treat this cancer is to go out-of-state and out of my HMO network for a new treatment called a 'Hot Chemo Wash.' This treatment sounds barbaric to me. Plus, it would cost me at least $30,000.00 out-of-pocket because my insurance probably won't cover any of it. Dr. Rodriguez is adamant that this is my only chance for survival. I called the specialist's office to find out the details. The person I spoke with was so awful to me. According to her, if I do not have this procedure immediately, I will be looking at a miserable life of constant surgery to keep removing tumors that keep popping up until I die within 2-3 years."

He touches my hand reassuringly. "I have a wonderful, local colon surgeon who I work with. He does an average of three of these surgeries a day... I'll tell you what, when you are sixty-five years old, you and I are going to make a phone call together to that specialist's office and tell them they are full of shit."

I hug him and thank him for being there for me and for fighting for my survival.

As pleased as I am that Dr. Roman has faith in his colon surgeon, I am still bothered by Dr. Rodriguez's insistence that no one locally is qualified and I must have the Hot Chemo Wash. I then go on to tell Dr. Roman about Dr. Rodriguez's strange offer to learn how to do this intricate surgery himself via virtual guidance from the specialist. I tell Dr. Roman that I have an upcoming appointment with Dr. Rodriguez. I also relay to him that Dr. Rodriguez was my rock during my breast cancer treatments, so his opinion is valued and carries some weight.

Dr. Roman is curious that my breast surgeon is requesting this meeting. He prods me, "Go. Listen to what he has to say, there's no harm in that. In the meantime, let's get you an appointment with Dr. Kay as soon as possible. I really think you will like him." Dr. Roman then introduces me to Bianca, a beautiful black woman with green eyes.

Bianca books the appointment with the colon doctor right then and there and tells me they will also take care of getting the referral. WOW, I am blown away! This office is amazing! I am so used to doing all this myself. I hug and thank everyone as I float out the door.

## July 15, 2009

As I wait in Dr. Rodriguez's lobby, my thoughts race:

*The doctors that were so competent treating my first cancer seem to be panicking now. I do trust Dr. Roman, but I cannot imagine that Dr. Rodriguez would steer me in such a wrong direction. I can't shake the feeling that Dr. Rodriguez is right about the Hot Chemo Wash but I am also feeling pressure from him… I hope our meeting today brings clarity.*

As soon as he enters the room, I explain to him that I've switched oncologists and Dr. Roman is recommending a local colon surgeon. He asks me the name of that surgeon and I reluctantly tell him. He repeats his bizarre offer. "Yes, I know Dr. Kay. If you are going to him, you may as well have me do the surgery instead."

*Really… Really? You're still pushing that?*

*Why is he totally dismissing my other treatment options. I feel he is too adamant about performing the Hot Chemo Wash himself.*

*How can he really believe I am better off with him learning this procedure for the first time on me? How could this be a better option for me than with someone whose specialty is treating appendix and colon cancer? It feels as though there is more more behind his strange offer …why doesn't he want me to explore other options? I don't really care what his motives are… at this very moment, my decision becomes clear. I want to run out of his office and never look back…*

I grab my purse and lunge for the door.

### August 10, 2009

My mom goes with me to meet Dr. Kay. We both really like this guy! He confidently conveys that this is his specialty and he does not agree that the Hot Chemo Wash is the only way to treat this cancer. He explains that he can do the surgery laparoscopically and, therefore, there will be minimal recovery time. Just as I am starting to calm down, he warns me of a small chance that I may need a colostomy bag for three months.

The thought of this keeps me up at night. The level of anxiety I am repeatedly subjected to is relentless and almost unbearable. I simply do not have the skills to cope. I wonder if anyone does. The worst part about cancer is not knowing what your quality of life would be if you survive.

### August 18, 2009

I meet with Dr Roman today.

"Dr. Roman, I have been through so much hell, I am so tired of all of this." My respect for him challenges me to be my best self. I hear my own whining and I don't like it, but I can't help myself. "I am still so weak and sick from the first cancer, I don't know how much more I can take. Just don't bother waking me up from the surgery if I need a colostomy bag on top of everything else."

He looks me in the eye and says, "Dr. Kay does three of these surgeries a day. You are in good hands, you won't need a bag."

I gaze at him as if I am a small, frightened child, even though he's probably younger than I am. *You need to promise me that I won't need a bag.*

He reads my mind, extending his hand, "Do you want to shake on this?"

"Yes."

He once again confidently states, "You will not need a bag…I promise."

"I believe you," I sigh.

I give permission to Dr. Roman and Dr. Kay to proceed with the surgery. It feels so good to finally make this decision.

Later that night I can't get this out of my head:

*Why on earth would my breast surgeon offer to do this surgery himself for the first time on me, with only virtual guidance, rather than advise me to go to a colon surgeon specialist who does three of these surgeries a day?*

# CHAPTER 11

# The Surgery

## September 2, 2009 / Surgery day

Fifteen minutes before my procedure, as I am lying in my pre-op bed surrounded by my loved ones, Dr. Kay approaches me with a solemn look on his face and announces, "I've consulted with many experts on your type of cancer. They are all in agreement that your surgery needs to be an open right hemi-colectomy, not a laparoscopic procedure. The surgery needs to be much more extensive, therefore, much more risk is involved. You will have an incision from your chest to your pelvic bone; I will be taking multiple biopsies and removing many lymph nodes."

Still lying on the pre-op bed, I am trying to digest this frightening new development. With no time to think it through, he hands me a liability form which makes my terror even worse. "I need you to sign this medical release form authorizing me to do the surgery and acknowledging that I have explained all of the risks to you."

This update is surreal and puts me in a horrified state of panic. Absolute terror encompasses my entire being as I am placed on the cold, steel gurney and wheeled away from my loved ones, not knowing if I will ever be okay again.

◀——◇——▶

I wake up from the surgery and see George's clear, sparkling, blue eyes looking down on me. He jubilantly says, "Julie, we have auspicious news! Thankfully, there are no visible signs that the cancer has spread." The loving expression on his face warms my heart.

We just have to wait for the final pathology to come back from the multiple biopsies that were taken during the surgery.

I am then moved into the Intensive Care Unit, ICU. My surgeon explains that he likes to have all of his patients closely monitored overnight after major surgery.

Not long after being in ICU, I am beginning to itch, and it is getting pretty uncomfortable. A nurse comes to check on me at about 1:00 a.m.

I tell her about the itching and ask for some Benadryl.

"Do you **really** want me to disturb your doctor at this hour? He has an early surgery at 6:00 a.m?" She lays on the guilt.

I ask, "Do you really have to bother him just for Benadryl?"

She snaps back, "Benadryl is not on your chart. I cannot authorize anything that is not on your chart."

"I guess it can wait until the morning."

**Big mistake!**

The itching gets more and more unbearable and I now have large, red, hive-like welts all over me. As each minute slowly creeps by, I am so uncomfortable that I am unable to sleep at all. This itching is driving me crazy!

There is nothing in the ICU to distract me such as a TV or radio, so I just watch the clock on the cold, gray wall creep along, minute-by-minute, second-by-second. No one ever comes back to check on me for the rest of the night.

*I really wish I was allowed to have my cell phone in here, I would call the hospital and ask to speak to someone in the ICU, "Help! I need help! I am in Bed 2 and I really need Benadryl!"*

After an agonizing night, I finally make it to the morning, but I am in a frantic state. The "House Doctor" comes in to finally check on me. I verbally jump on him, "I have been up all night! I can't believe no one in this hospital could give me Benadryl! I am itching like crazy! Where is my doctor?"

"Is there something **else** wrong with you?"

I am completely jarred by his question. "What?"

"You are behaving irrationally. I am asking you if there is something **else** wrong with you?"

I study his face and glare angrily into his eyes. It takes me a minute to realize what he is insinuating and I become outraged. "Oh My God! You think that I am crazy, don't you? I need a phone! I need to call someone to get me the hell out of here!"

Once my doctor is contacted, I am admitted to a private room and am treated like a human being again. I tell my nurses about my awful experience in the ICU and they say I should report what happened to the hospital administration. I just want to forget about it. I have enough problems!

## September 7, 2009

I am home from the hospital and it has been a week since my surgery. The staples are doing a poor job of holding my abdomen together. I can't look at my torso. My skin is so swollen and puckered, it makes me squeamish to look at it. I would make a good prop in the movie *Texas Chainsaw Massacre*.

I am uncharacteristically nonchalant about the impending huge scar. I am just so happy to have a positive outcome from the surgery. Gratitude trumps vanity.

I am told I can't drive for at least two weeks, so my mom takes me to get my stitches out. I treat myself to a few extra pain pills to help me venture out of the house for the first time since the surgery.

As my mom and I enter the colon surgeon's office, I can feel the entire room turn to look, probably wondering which one of us has the colorectal problem.

I pretend it's her. This requires a lot of calculating on my part. I use my elderly mother as a crutch so I can stand upright, but I am trying to convey that **she** needs **my** help. She hasn't yet realized what I am doing, so she's not cooperating with my clever ruse.

I desperately try to suppress an inappropriate case of the giggles, which only makes the urge to laugh stronger. Between the extra dose of pain meds kicking in, combined with the good news that the cancer probably has not spread, I morph into a silly, middle-school girl on a field trip.

The front desk asks to see my driver's license and insurance information, which makes my charade with my mother difficult to keep up.

I announce, "Mom, how about if I bring that to the desk for you?"

She splashes cold water on my elaborate plan and loudly corrects me, "What are you talking about, honey? They don't want to see **my** ID, they want to see **yours**?" My mother believes the solution to her hearing loss is simply to talk louder. As a result, I am so busted!

As we sit and wait, I notice the room is unusually quiet. I suppose there are some conversations that are just too awkward to start…

*"Hello. So what brings you here today, hemorrhoids?"*

An attractive man in his twenties staggers in, looking too young to need a colon surgeon. My mom is way ahead of me. She leans over to whisper discretely in my ear, but instead screams, "What the hell did he do last night to land himself in here?" I can't control my giggles.

Our childish antics quickly get us escorted to a private room.

As I glance around the claustrophobic cubicle, I notice odd machines with long hoses lining the wall. I can't help also noticing the numerous lubricant tubes. My imagination does not do me any favors. Suddenly nothing is funny anymore.

A stocky, sour-faced woman in scrubs enters the room to remove my staples. I don't learn her name, but she looks like a Helga as she approaches the examination table.

"Lay down," she orders.

I can sense Helga's impatience with me because I am taking too long to maneuver my body into the proper position.

"Hold still. Stop moving and it won't hurt so much." I squirm with fearful anticipation. She quickly and skillfully removes my staples and marches out the door. I hear her soldier footsteps fading down the hallway.

The lightness I experienced in the lobby is now replaced with a lump in my throat.

I am not wearing a watch, but can tell by the pain returning around my incision that we have been waiting at least two hours to see Dr. Kay. As he finally enters the room, I study his expression for clues. The optimism I had earlier keeps subsiding. I try to remember if his face always looks so melancholy or does he have bad news? I remind myself, *if he was a people- person he probably would have chosen a different vocation.*

Before I say "Hello" or "Thanks for doing the surgery" I blurt out, "Did the pathology come back from all the biopsies?"

He does a "180" and mumbles, "Let me see if the results are back." At least his dark expression has nothing to do with my results. He doesn't even know what they are.

Staring catatonically at the hoses in the room for another hour, my mom and I are too nervous to speak. We are tucked away in yet another small room. I am perspiring through yet another paper-thin, white vest, waiting for yet another doctor to reveal my fate. This never gets any easier.

We eventually open the door, just in case he forgot about us and went to lunch. My mom breaks the silence and asks, "Think we should leave?"

"Mom, I really need to know if I am okay."

Finally, Helga marches in with my biopsy results in hand. I involuntarily shake with terror as I attempt to read her demeanor. She unenthusiastically mumbles, "Oh, you are cancer-free."

"Excuse me, can you please repeat what you just said?"

She raises her eyebrows in defiance at having to repeat herself. She then overly- enunciates each word to condescendingly indicate how I am inconveniencing her. "I... Said... You ... Are ... Clear."

My mother and I instinctively grab each other's hands and cry with joy. Even though I am in excruciating pain because my meds have completely worn off, I manage to raise my body from the examination table and give Helga a big hug. She recoils as I reach out to her. I take delight in the thought that I make her confront her own coldness.

I ask her if Dr. Kay wants to talk to me.

"I don't think so."

As my mom and I drive home we discuss the oddness of the appointment. "You would think that a surgeon who frequently deals with cancer would love those moments when he can actually give good news."

The next day I will find out the truth, but that night, I sleep soundly under the illusion that I am finished with this nightmare.

# CHAPTER 12

# The Decision

**September 8, 2009**

I stopped taking the pain pills because they have messed up my stomach. I am an angry ball of human suffering, but I still have to drag myself to another doctor's appointment. I can't walk, let alone drive, so mom has to pick me up again.

She is wearing the same shirt she wore yesterday. "This is my good-luck shirt. We had good news yesterday, so I wanted to wear it again."

Our fear has made us uncharacteristically superstitious. "Honey are you in a lot of pain?" she asks.

"Yeah, I had to stop taking the pain meds."

"What, hon?"

"I can't take the pills anymore."

"What, hon?"

"I...can't... take... pills." I snap.

My poor, sweet mother is the unlucky recipient of my misplaced anger. Her hearing deficit is too much for me to cope with today. I become mean like Helga and hate myself for it. How can my exterior demeanor be in such conflict with my heart? I'm so grateful and feel such love for my mom.

She's been by my side through every nuance of my illnesses. I couldn't have gotten through all of this without her. Yet, I can't control my caustic demeanor with her.

For a brief second, I think about Helga and feel compassion for her. *Perhaps she was in some kind of pain that caused her to be so cold to us yesterday. Nah, who am I kidding? She's just a bitch who needs to find a different career.*

As we arrive at Dr. Roman's office, I'm clutching a thick sweater to my abdomen in hopes that it will dull the stabbing pain. I'm wearing this oversized, ugly, blue muumuu with loud, annoying flowers—the only thing in my closet I can just throw over my head. I can't lift my legs enough to put on pants, so it's either this dress or my nightgown. Wearing a muumuu with sneakers is out of the question, so I suffer wearing one-inch heels after major colon surgery. I somehow believe the medical profession will treat me better if I pull myself together and look as cute as possible. It's getting harder and harder to pull this off. I'm sure I look pitiful to even try.

My heart sinks with disappointment as the oncology waiting room is so crowded. I just want to go home and pull the covers over my head. For the first time since my cancer journey began, I feel that I'm part of the pessimistic, sickly, energy that surrounds me in these different waiting rooms....I am now one of the pasty, disintegrating skeletons. I can no longer pretend this isn't happening to me. I look and feel as bad as everyone else.

This is the worst day possible for Dr. Roman to be backlogged. I keep re-positioning myself, trying to get comfortable in the small, hard chairs, but I can't find a position, sitting or standing, that makes the pain tolerable.

When we are finally put into one of those claustrophobic cubicles, Dr. Roman walks by and nods his head at me, smiling,

"You're next." I like him so much I forget to be grouchy. His soft leather shoes and warm expression lighten the room. I remember Dr. Scary's shoes, hard and commanding. I have never been particularly observant of footwear before, perhaps it is the result of sitting on all of the examination tables, with my face staring at the floor!

He enters the room smiling and talking about my surgery results. "We have the best news possible! Great news! No signs of cancer. As of now, you are cancer-free! Here are the statistics for your type of cancer. If you do not get chemo there is a 35-45% chance that your cancer will come back. If you do get chemo that drops to 22%. You have been through so much already, the choice has to be yours." His penetrating gaze indicates that he knows he's relaying information that I do not want to hear. His demeanor is a complex yet sturdy mixture of physician, psychologist, mathematician, and wonderful friend.

This news, once again, knocks the air out of me. The room spins. I take a moment to regain my composure. *No wonder my colon surgeon avoided me yesterday.* Without saying a word, we carefully gauge each other's reactions. In my head, I am calculating the difference between 45 % and 22 %. *Is it really worth putting my body through more chemo for 23% ?*

My eyes drift to the floor to avoid his. My father's voice is in my head, *"Julie, I forbid it! I absolutely forbid it!"* I am leaning heavily towards "no."

I look up at Dr. Roman, ready to factor in his assessment. His poker face is imperceptible. Our stalemated silence penetrates the room. He conveys no sense of urgency to get to his next patient which I find so humbling as I recall the crowded waiting room. My emotions are confused.

I once read somewhere that you could not feel gratitude and fear at the same time. Not true. Despite my overwhelming anxiety, I experience tremendous gratitude embarking on this journey with him, instead of with Dr. Scary.

My mother can't take the silence and blurts out, "Dr. Roman, tell us what to do."

"If you were my sister, you wouldn't be given a choice. You would absolutely be getting the chemo."

I point to my hair and make a face that conveys, "*Again?*"

He looks sad. "Yes, you will lose your hair again."

"I have a stupid question…"

"No question is stupid."

"This will be the third time I lose my hair. At some point will it stop growing back?"

"No. It will always grow back." He smiles at my concern. "I will give you a few days to decide. Call me Friday, this has to be your choice."

I realize how brilliantly he handles this. If he just demands, "You need chemo," I would not take ownership but would feel this was forced upon me. Instead, it becomes my choice. He gives me the odds and lets me decide.

*Only I can answer the question…is it worth it to me, or have I had enough?*

# CHAPTER 13

# This Chemo is Rough!

### October 10th, 2009

I'm on the fourth day of my new chemo regimen. So far it's not that bad, just this weird sensitivity to cold in my mouth. It's hard to describe. It feels like my taste buds turn into pin pricks. I ate ice cream yesterday just to see what would happen and my tongue became briefly paralyzed. I won't try that again.

I seem to be handling everything okay. I have some stomach cramping, my face feels tender around my cheek bones, and I had the hiccups for hours yesterday.

### October 15, 2009

While drinking my morning coffee, trying to ignore the acidic metallic taste, I try to plan my day. I am a week out from chemo and want to get some errands done.

Feeling weak and a little disoriented, I venture out anyway. I only have two stops, first, to the bank drive-thru, then to the grocery store to pick up a few frozen dinners, as I am far too weak to cook. *Oh, who am I kidding, even before cancer, I never cooked.*

When I get to the bank drive-thru, I rummage through my purse looking for a deposit slip. I meekly ask the teller through the speaker, "Can you please send me a deposit slip?"

"No, you have to come inside."

"Do I really have to come in the bank and stand in line? I am going through chemo and I am really weak and sick today. Please, is there anything you can do to help me?"

"There is nothing I can do, you need to wait in line like everyone else."

I enter the bank and follow the red, velvet rope indicating the end of the line. I sneer at the pink ribbons plastered all around the bank, "We Support Breast Cancer Awareness." *Damn, wrong cancer, I had breast cancer last year!*

Hot flashes drench my being as I suddenly feel like I have been transported to a long line at Disney World in the excruciating summer heat. Reality feels altered. Is everyone stoned or is it my imagination that I am in a time warp? Everything is moving so slowly...what the hell is wrong with me? My mental clarity is deteriorating as each person is called to the next available teller. By the time I get to the window, I can barely speak or stand upright but manage to communicate effectively enough to get some cash for the grocery store. Woozy, I almost knock over one of the pink ribbon banners on my way out. Angrily, I mumble to myself,

*Spare me the pink ribbons! If you are going to plaster them all around, how about a little compassion when I tell you I have cancer and I'm too weak to stand in a long line?*

My next stop is the grocery store, but as I get in my car I realize something is really wrong with me. I feel dizzy and disoriented. I think it's my blood sugar and need to eat.

I manage to make my way into the nearest deli I can find. As I enter, I must look like a lost cast member from The Walking Dead. I am barely able to focus and talk.

I drag myself to the counter and weakly mumble, " I am going through chemo, I have to sit down, but I'd like a bagel and some orange juice, please."

I must have terrified the waitress. She escorted me to a nearby table and said, "Honey, you just have a seat. I'll bring that right to you."

As I wait for my bagel, I debate having them call for an ambulance. The room is spinning and I feel as though my body and mind are not connected to each other. It is the weirdest sensation.

After I eat, I convince myself it was just my blood sugar and I really need to get some food in the house. As I enter the grocery store, I head right to the frozen food section just to pick up a couple of quick meals. I immediately get that weird, disoriented feeling again.

I make my way to to the counter and explain that I am going through chemo and having a rough day. The woman behind the counter is wonderful. She has me sit while she checks out my groceries.

I rely on her honesty as I hand her a wad of cash.

"Are you ok to drive?"

"I think so." I lie.

I know I should not get behind the wheel, but I desperately want to get home to call Dr. Roman's office to determine if I need to go to the hospital.

I call George and tell him he needs to stay on the phone with me until I get home. I try to explain the feeling that I am outside of my own head and I need a connection to someone I love to talk me home.

I am only a few blocks from my house but it feels like I am in a foreign country. I don't recognize anything. I question if I am driving in the right direction. *Who am I?*

*Where am I? Am I going to die now? Is this what it feels like to lose my mind?*

George mistakenly thinks I am having a panic attack. I am too scared to correct him and explain it has something to do with the chemo.

Even in my altered state, I understand that George is in denial about what I am going through. He is trying to downplay my symptoms, not acknowledging that I have entered this terrifying world of cancer that no one I know can coach me through.

I barely make it home and immediately call Dr. Roman's office…the nurse I speak with is very calm and un-alarmed.

"Sarah, what is going on? I feel disoriented and out of my own head, I can't even describe it. Am I making sense to you right now?"

"Julie, listen to me. Are your lips dry?"

"Yes, as a matter of fact they are so dry they actually have scabs on them."

"You are going to be okay, you are severely dehydrated from the chemo. You need to drink, drink, drink water, no coffee. If you do drink coffee while on this chemo, you need to have three glasses of water to counteract the dehydration that coffee causes. I will talk to Dr. Roman about setting up a hydration drip after each treatment so this doesn't happen again "

I follow her instructions and within an hour I begin to feel better. I thought the breast cancer treatments were harsh, but this scare is different. I feel like I almost died today.

# CHAPTER 14

# Help from my New Friends!

**November 15, 2009**

Imagine a place that you fear from afar—somewhere that is so terrifying and unfamiliar to you that you will avoid any reference to it. Throughout my life, I avoided any movie, song, or book about someone battling cancer.

Then, suddenly, this place I feared becomes part of my calendar, every other Thursday. Ironically, for the rest of my life, I will be able to walk into any chemo room, anywhere in the world and feel at home.

At Dr. Roman's, a small group of us that have our chemo at the same time are becoming friends.

"Hey, Julie, I saved you a seat." My new friend Shirley enthusiastically gestures her hand to the chair next to her.

"Thanks, Shirley!" Sometimes that one line, "I saved you a seat," is all we say to each other for five or six hours as we drift in and out of lucidity. Her warmth and humor make this bearable. I feel love sitting next to me. Our friendship has grown past the chemo room. We often talk on the phone at night, allowing each other to vent, but it is our laughter that pulls us through these dire circumstances.

Shirley has advanced, stage 4 breast cancer that has spread to her liver and bones. Her neuropathy is even worse than mine. She wears the recommended heavy, black, monstrous shoes that I should be wearing, but I would rather fall on my ass several times a day.

The third member of our group is Cathy. She called me at home one evening and talked my ear off. This is the first time in my life I am truly learning to set limits with people. I am so weak that I have no tolerance or energy to be anything but brutally authentic. I find Cathy's conversation completely exhausting as she is trying to convince me that my treatment will be so much easier if I convert and become a Jehovah's Witness.

"Look, I like you and I want us to be friends. I am not going to become a Jehovah's Witness and you need to back off. Having said that, we have something great forming with Shirley at chemo. I look forward to seeing you guys and laughing with you. I think it helps us all." She promises not to mentioned it again. We are unlikely friends but being in the foxhole with her is fun. She's loud and inappropriately critical of the entire medical staff, including Dr. Roman. She is like a bull in a china shop. This is off-putting at first, but we soon learn Cathy's just full of angry, hot air that's easily diffused with laughter. She often winks at us when she's giving the nurses a hard time, indicating she isn't really as angry as she is coming across. We don't want the nurses to think we agree with Cathy, but she's part of our group so we accept our fate, knowing we are often lumped together as troublemakers. Actually, most of the nurses love us, except for one humorless nurse who demands total silence and our utmost perfect behavior during chemo.

There is one day in particular that seals our fate. We are joking about the gross side effects of chemo, particularly the unbearable constipation. There's a very lady-like and delicate woman who starts the conversation that day. She whispers softly, "Do you guys have a problem with constipation after the chemo?"

"Oh, God, yes! It's like trying to pass a watermelon!" Shirley quips back.

Our petite new friend admits, " I took three laxatives last night. I got so excited because I felt some rumbling. Then, after all that commotion, do you know what pops out? An M&M- sized little dot!"

Our laughter echoes through the sterile hallway.

"Shush! You are disturbing the patients trying to rest."

Apparently we laugh too much for the sour nurse who we quickly nickname Nurse Ratched. She separates us, treating us like middle-school troublemakers in the cafeteria.

On my way out, one of the other patients calls me over. "You guys make me laugh every time you are here. Thank you."

We are under no illusions about where we are or what we are facing, but there is nothing funnier or more comforting than facing our fears together. We are all trying to be brave for the people in our lives. By contrast, what freedom it is to be able to just be honest about all of it. There are brief moments when the chemo room feels like Sunday morning at home.... the sun splashing over half-read newspapers sprawled on the chairs set up for patients' loved ones, the aroma of fresh coffee flowing through the air, and familiar faces from two weeks ago smiling at me as I settle in for the long day ahead.

When I went through breast cancer I didn't have much of an appetite and lost about ten pounds. This chemo is completely different. Dr. Roman explains, "Eat whatever you crave, which will be greasy, fattening foods. You need the calories, so don't worry about your weight." If I don't eat large and heavy meals every few hours, I suffer withdrawal symptoms like a crack addict, shaking and sweating, alleviated only by gorging on the next large, greasy and fattening meal.

Not surprisingly, I gain the ten pounds I lost during the first cancer and add another ten, madly craving chocolate, pizza and greasy burgers the whole time. The unfortunate aspect is that every time I eat, within minutes I am clutching my stomach and running to the nearest bathroom. My appetite is so ravenous that it has a mind of its own and does not care about the consequences.

## December 31, 2009

We are planning a special day at chemo. We can't call it a New Year's Eve celebration because Cathy is a Jehovah's Witness, but nobody really cares what we call it…we just want to feel normal.

Cathy brings homemade cheesecake and fresh coffee. I pretend to enjoy the coffee even though it tastes like metal.

My contribution to our party is called "Ooey Gooey Cake." I have a friend who is a wonderful pastry chef and these cakes are her specialty. I bring in several for the patients getting chemo that day, and several for the nurses. We quickly go through our stash, so Cathy demands pieces from the nurses' stash. Every half-hour she asks a different nurse for some cake and plays it off that she never got a piece. It becomes funnier and funnier as the day goes on. The entire chemo room is in on our joke. For a fleeting moment it feels like a real holiday.

# CHAPTER 15

# What do I do Now?

### March 30, 2010

Oh My God! So tired. I can't write while in this frame of mind. I don't recognize my own voice.

### April 8, 2010

I finished my chemo three weeks ago. I am still exhausted, but there is a deeper concern that I am suppressing. My entire life revolves around managing my side effects and the world goes on without me. There is something Rip Van Winklesque about this whole thing.

I am almost fifty years old. My appearance has changed, the world around me has changed and yet the hardest realization is that I am no longer a cog in the wheel of life. I gradually move all my business suits to the back of my closet. I am too tired, frail and sick to care about anything. I do not have any faith in my life expectancy…I am living with constant fear that one of the cancers will come back.

For over two years I have been undergoing treatments. I have been unable to work. I still go to my Lady Fit group, but I can no longer teach the class. In fact, I can't even drive myself. One of my friends picks me up and takes me. The ladies remember the routines, so most of the time I sit in a chair in the corner just to be out and amongst my friends.

Before George moved in with me, I had paid off my modest mortgage. I was still healthy and wanted to take the financial pressure off when I left my corporate job. I had reached a point in my life where I was financially stable enough to take a risk and pursue a more fulfilling career path.

God laughs while we make plans!

Now, I am watching everything I have worked for trickle down each month. I can't financially support myself and it is heart-wrenching for me.

I am rapidly depleting my life savings. I have no income. George is not in a position to support me, nor would I expect this. Through the years we rarely talk about money, but early on we made an agreement that we each would pay half of the bills. Our relationship is based on a strong philosophy we both share, that we are two self-sufficient people who do not place unrealistic demands on one another. I feel like I am betraying him if I start to turn into a very different kind of woman…one with completely different financial expectations of him because I am sick.

I knew George had been financially devastated by a bad divorce. He is such a kind-hearted and responsible man that the most important aspect of his divorce was to uphold his relationship with his daughters. As a result, he was never able to recover financially and lives paycheck to paycheck. We are together now almost fourteen years and he is still paying alimony. My feminist brain just can't wrap my head around this. He is paying alimony longer than he was married. When friends of mine need a good divorce lawyer, I ask them one question, "Do you care about your ex-husband at all?" If they answer "No," I refer them to George's ex-wife's lawyer.

## April 17, 2010

All of my medical co-pays and deductibles are adding up. Every time I go for a test or scan it is between $250.00 and $500.00 out-of-pocket. My radiation treatments are a few thousand dollars **with** health insurance. I don't know what people do if they are uninsured. I guess the sad truth is—they die. I am scraping by, watching my retirement fund dwindle. I am looking at one of my medical bills, trying to understand what chemo would cost if I didn't have insurance. It is hard to decipher the bill, but I think it was around $20,000 per round. I have had thirty two rounds. Who on earth could afford this without insurance? That's just for the chemo, not including the rest of the drugs and tests.

When I feel well enough to get out of the house, I do not allow myself to spend any money on non-necessities, and for the first time in my life, I only shop at thrift stores. My corporate buddies would cringe to see what my life has been reduced to in such a short period of time. I can't believe how quickly I am going through my life's savings.

## April 27, 2010

My last treatment was five weeks ago.

Everyone asks with an eager smile, "How are you feeling?"

I know they want me to say "Great!"

I am as far from great as anyone can get. I feel so much pressure from everyone around me to "bounce back" and be Julie again.

Yes, I am alive and I am grateful for that, but I feel ancient. Every bone in my body hurts. I suppose it's how someone feels recovering from being hit by a bus, then crawling into the street and getting hit by a bigger bus over and over and over.

My hands and feet burn as if they are on fire. My brain doesn't work. I can't read more than a few words nor comprehend what I have read. I am so, so tired— a fatigue that is never alleviated by sleep. It is a fatigue that all of the positive thoughts and gratitude for being alive cannot make any better. There are periods of time where my vision becomes distorted and I feel disoriented. Constant and painful stomach cramps grip me as my system tries to regulate after all the trauma. I either burn up with a hot flash or I am cold and wet when the heat has passed. In a moment of self-pity, I ponder if there is a God, is he punishing me…for what…because I didn't breed? I didn't pray?

I cannot talk my way out of this, I cannot think positive thoughts and focus on the fact that I am alive because, in truth, I am not really alive. Sadly, I don't know what to do to rebuild some kind of a quality of life. How do I put myself back together physically, mentally, emotionally, financially?

I have been battling cancer from October, 2007 to April, 2010.

*Is Cancer winning?*

# CHAPTER 16

# The Letter

### April 28, 2010

Just when I am wondering if I will ever be able to bounce back from everything that has happened, I get another brutal blow. I receive a letter in the mail that my health insurance is being cancelled. "We regret to inform you that we are no longer providing coverage in your area"...*nothing personal but we don't give a shit if you die!*

### April 29, 2010

I roll out of bed, the room is spinning..it hurts to lift my head...I take a few sips of coffee and begin to get severe stomach cramps. I spend the next few hours going from the bed to the bathroom. I pick up the letter I received yesterday which includes a list of insurance companies to call for possible coverage. This task is monumental. I think to myself, *Julie, just start with one call.*

"Hello, I am calling because my insurance company referred me to you for health insurance."

"Hi, my name is Debbie. I'll be happy to help you." After the perfunctory questions about my age, weight, and benign medical conditions, I wait for it, here it comes. "Have you ever had cancer?"

"Yes."

"What kind?"

I respond, "Which time?"

I hear an audible gasp, "I'm sorry, Ms. Klein, I actually thought I heard you say, 'which time?' " She laughs nervously.

"Yes, you heard me correctly. I have had breast and appendix cancer."

Her friendly voice turns icy. "I'm going to have to put you on hold. This may take a while."

I close my eyes and lie on the bed. I actually welcome being put on hold so I can rest awhile.

She gets back on the line and coldly recites, "You need to call this special number for people in your situation."

⬦

"Hello, this is Suzy from (the name sounds suspicious, something like Hope-Care-Eternal- Group-Unlimited).

"Hi, Suzy. My name is Julie. I need health insurance and I have two pre-existing cancers."

"Well, you are such a fighter." With a perky voice she exclaims, "It just wasn't in God's plan for you to die yet, was it? Let me see what I can do for you." I hear her clicking endlessly on her computer. "Okay, Ms. Klein, we have a special plan just for you!" Suzy starts to talk so fast that I can barely understand what she is relaying. She begins to quote plans with astronomical numbers. "Let's see, I have a plan for a little over $1000.00 a month. It is for catastrophic care only. You also will have very high deductibles, plus there are exclusions on the plan, meaning because of your pre-existing history, they wouldn't cover any care related to either cancer."

My heart sinks, "Suzy, is that the best you can do for me? I can't afford even close to this amount; I am not even able to work part-time. I don't know what to do."

She lowers her voice, "I'm going to be honest with you, Ms. Klein. You seem like a really nice person. I'm going to tell you a secret, but you can't say you heard it from me." She whispers, "I could lose my job if they heard me tell you this. Why don't you file for bankruptcy and apply for welfare, then your healthcare will be free. Do you have more than $2,000.00 in total assets? Do you own your own home?"

I explain to Suzy, "Yes, I do own my own home, and although I am not a wealthy person, I do have a retirement fund that is more than $2,000.00. As I am listening to your numbers, I can see I will go through what money I have very quickly. I don't know what to do."

Suzy's voice is now filled with compassion. "Here's what you need to do...put all of your assets in someone else's name and apply for Medicaid. That is the only way someone like you can get affordable healthcare now that you have had two cancers. Remember, you can't tell anyone I told you this or I will lose my job."

I hang up the phone in deep despair. The thought of giving away my assets to go on welfare is incomprehensible. I can't do that. I curl up into a fetal position on my bed and cry for the first time since my diagnosis. I thought I was broken by the second cancer, but this is even more shattering.

### April 30, 2010

I wake up, see the letter on the end table by my bed and start to feel rage.

*I don't understand how this could happen to me…I have never been without insurance my entire adult life! Even when I have changed jobs and had to decide whether to risk being without coverage or pay the higher COBRA rates, I always opted to pay the higher rates. I didn't want to risk getting hurt or sick and not have health insurance. I am so damn responsible…if this can happen to me, this can happen to anybody!*

*What is wrong with this picture?*

*I have paid into the insurance system for thirty five years without ever even asking for so much as an aspirin, then, when I actually start to need some care, I get a letter in the mail… sorry sucker, we milked you while you were healthy but now you have to fend for yourself!*

*I feel like I am being thrown away because I am no longer cost effective.*

<hr />

Like a wounded child, my first instinct is to call my mom for comfort.

"I don't know what to do, Mom."

"Sweetheart, you have been through so much. I wish I could take this worry away from you. I can try to help you, but we are not wealthy people."

"Mom. I could never ask that of you. Besides, you and I both know that a couple rounds of chemo would bankrupt us both. I refuse to take you down with me. Even if I pay $1000.00 every month, it still won't cover most of my care because of my pre-existing issues. The insurance will only cover a new health condition. I have to tell you, I have tried to be so strong and handle this myself. Up until this point I have taken what has been thrown at me and just dealt with it. You know how self-sufficient I have always been. I don't know how to handle this, I don't know what to do! I have a few more numbers to call on the list my insurance company gave me, but I have lost faith that there is anything out there for me."

"Honey, I read something about a high risk pool...What about that?"

"That may be an option as a last resort. The problem with that is I have to be uninsured for six months before I can qualify, then it takes a month to get enrolled. The year after my cancer diagnosis is really critical to catch a recurrence early. I can't be un-insured during this critical time in my follow up care!"

### May 3, 2010

Monday morning, I wake up in a cold sweat, gripped by anxiety. I need to finish making the phone calls to all of the insurance companies on the list I was sent. This is inhumane. I am too sick to do this. My doctors tell me how important it is to avoid stress and remain calm. I can't even function enough to go to the grocery store without assistance, yet I somehow now have to be my own advocate and find medical insurance that will cover two pre-existing aggressive cancers. What a joke!

### June 5, 2010

I have now called every company on this list. No one has affordable coverage for me. I continue to be shocked, devastated and so, so tired.

### July 10, 2010

I see a commercial on TV promising healthcare coverage for people like me with pre-existing conditions, "even if you have been turned down everywhere else."

I am so desperate that I call the number. By now I know what questions to ask but almost get sucked into buying a sub-standard policy because the sales people are so convincing. The person I spoke with is either totally comfortable lying through his teeth about the benefits I will actually receive, or he is kept in the dark on purpose so he won't know he is selling me a sub-standard policy.

Meanwhile, to my absolute horror, I see well-dressed, well-insured congressmen in suits on TV, trying to persuade the American people that access to affordable healthcare is a privilege, not a right. I scream at the TV, "I am not asking for free healthcare, you idiots! I just want people like me, with a history of cancer, not to be priced out of the market! Why should I have to lose everything because I got sick! Why should I have to die because I can't afford healthcare!" My angry screams fall on deaf ears…I am yelling at an empty box and no one hears me.

## July 15, 2010

Dread looms inside me. The terror is not just about either of the cancers returning. If I do survive, I will drain my life's savings and security within months. My employment prospects are even more dire than I originally understood. I am an entirely different person with strange and invisible side effects. I feel like an unidentified species.

As I research my odd ailments, it's clear that conventional medicine has no answers to my very real limitations. In fact, I am encountering something quite shocking…the medical profession seems to be blowing me off. There's this uncomfortable feeling that my doctors are metaphorically rolling their eyes when I ask and ask and ask and ask, "What can I do to improve my quality of life? How am I supposed to work if I have no reading comprehension and I can only function for small intervals of time, needing total quiet for hours to recoup. I have an ongoing, exhausting fatigue unrelieved by sleep. What did all of that chemo do to my brain? Why is my nervous system so messed up? Why? Why? Why?"

### August 1, 2010

My only solution to my pressing health insurance and financial problems is to figure out a way to work toward full-time employment so I have a steady income with health insurance through my employer. This feels like such a steep, unrealistic mountain to climb. I have very real damage that was done to my body and nervous system that does not translate well to viable employment. I can't imagine performing in a job setting.

I am forced to rely on people who take pity on me because no one in his or her right mind would hire me or keep me on their payroll once they realize how messed up I am. I had many marketable skills and all have deteriorated beyond recognition. Keeping up with technology was never a strength of mine, but now that I have been in a chemo fog for years, the world has simply moved on without me.

In past management jobs I often conducted interviews, so I know what to look for in a viable job applicant. I can't imagine how I could get through the interview process and be hired now. I play out the interview questions in my head:

*"So, Ms. Klein, would you be able to work overtime if necessary?"*

*"Well, to be honest, I have about an hour of productivity a day, then my brain and my nervous system no longer function. In my defense, I think I am smarter than the general population during that hour before I completely lose it."*

"Ms. Klein, can you work in an environment that requires multi-tasking?"

"I use to be very good at multi-tasking. In a prior management role there was a constant line outside my office door and I quickly shifted gears from one employee's problems to the next. Unfortunately, since the chemo nerve damage, I become overwhelmed when there is more than one sensory input at a time. For example, if I am home and the phone rings the same time as the doorbell, my head spins and I can't answer either one."

I force myself to stop imagining these awful scenarios.

## August 12, 2010

One of my dearest friends, Susan, takes pity on me and offers to help. She manages a small women's clothing boutique that is experimenting with calling their customers regarding upcoming sales. No one on her staff wants to make these calls.

She offers me $8.00 an hour for approximately six hours a week to make phone calls. She realizes I can't work on a set schedule because I have to work around my physical limitations. I can make the calls at my convenience during business hours, as long as I can get through the call-list by the end of the week. Despite the fact that I am grateful for the opportunity to try working, I am under no illusions that this job is going to be able to lead me to self-sufficiency. However, it's a way to enter the work force and "test the waters" to see what I am capable of. It is also a plus that she is my friend and understands my health problems so I won't have to explain if I am not feeling well and have to leave.

It seems like a good place to start.

It takes about a half- hour to drive to the boutique. This eats up half of my day's energy before I even arrive.

When I get there, I sit in the back room on a hard, uncomfortable chair to make the calls. After about a half-hour my physical problems start kicking in. My back begins to ache and as I get more and more fatigued, my vision gets blurry and my ability to concentrate starts to deteriorate. The call-sheet that I am given becomes difficult to see. It is nearly impossible to line up the customer's name and contact information. As a result, I often call the same person twice, thinking that I have moved onto the next name. The nerve damage in my fingers, peripheral neuropathy, affects my ability to use the keypad on the phone and properly document my calls. I can't feel my fingers so I am not sure what keys I am hitting. I am calling wrong numbers as I feel more and more disoriented. Fatigue brings on hot flashes. I am drenched in sweat which is dripping all over the call-sheets.

My normally pleasant personality grows intolerant. I have to leave after only two hours because I am disoriented and worried that I won't be able to drive home. Driving there and back, I spend a total of an hour in the car for two hours of work. I am pushing my body beyond it's capacity but I will do anything to try to get back into the work force.

This job does not last more than a month, at which time Susan and I agree that I am not able to keep doing this.

### September 12, 2010

I now realize that I can't take care of myself. The truth is, I have been reluctant to think of asking for help. To do so breaks every rule and belief that I have held about my own self-sufficiency. My neighbor, watching my world crumble around me, has been urging me for months to apply for Social Security Disability. I finally am forced to agree. The last thing I want to do is to see myself as disabled. I don't know how to have a productive life without working. Yet, I have to face my reality that I need help supporting myself.

## October 20, 2010

Today I receive my second rejection letter from disability. "**We believe your ailments do not rise to the level of disability.**"

This letter is shocking to me.

Here I am beating myself up because over time I have been forced to reach the painful conclusion that I can't work and in an unsigned, bureaucratic form letter they are rejecting me because they believe I **can** work and just don't want to!

Has anyone on this "anonymous committee" ever had 32 rounds of chemo?

For days after receiving this letter I feel worthless and guilty. I feel like a failure. This letter triggers deep and dark emotional pain. It reflects my darkest fear of myself.

## October 25, 2010

In bed, depressed and hopeless, I bury my head under the covers. I have the TV on in the background and I hear an add for a prominent Disability Lawyer, "If your claim has been denied, we fight for your rights."

I drag myself out of bed and call the number. At first, the young voice on the other end of the phone warns me that they will not take my case unless they feel that I have a strong chance of winning.

"Why can't you work?" She prods.

"I have had two back-to-back stage 3 cancers, 32 rounds of chemo, multiple surgeries that leave me with chronic digestive issues. I have peripheral neuropathy in my hands and feet. I get debilitating fatigue and can only function for small amounts of time due to the damage to my nervous system from the years of chemo. I can't read…"

She interrupts me and briefly puts me on hold then quickly comes back, "We are accepting your case."

"What's next? When do I meet with the lawyer?"

"Not until your hearing date is set. What we need you to do now is to have all of your doctors fill out the forms that we are going to send you. We will collect all of your medical records and call you if we have any questions."

"Okay. What do you think my chances are?"

"I don't know."

"Can I speak to the lawyer representing me?"

"You are not assigned to a lawyer until you have a date for your hearing. For now, you just need to concentrate on getting your doctors to fill out the forms we send you."

# CHAPTER 17

# Dad's Cancer Comes Back

**November 2, 2010**

My concerns about my own dire situation have to temporarily take a back seat to an even worse tragedy. My dad's lymphoma is back with a vengeance. This time it's in his brain.

His dying wish is that I take him to the local library to vote. I'm still so weak, recovering from my own cancer, but I can't say no to him.

Anyone who does not know my father would wonder why he's so driven to vote in a mid-term election during the last few days, or possibly hours, of his life.

When he was healthy, there was always a sharp contrast between who my father was versus how my father looked. He was not big on personal grooming. My mother gave up trying to make him look presentable. It was not unusual to have his "plumber's crack" showing at Thanksgiving dinner. He often wore stained clothing and could have more than a few missed spots on his face from his haphazard attempt to shave. His thinning, disheveled hair had a wild Einstein-like quality, which made him look crazed at times when he was vehemently trying to make a point….until you really listened to what he had to say.

My father is the most brilliant person I know.

The cancer now is affecting his balance, speech, and coordination. He is too stubborn and proud to let us help him get dressed, so he is quite a sight to behold the day we enter the public library for him to vote. He needs a walker to get around, but he hasn't quite mastered it yet. He operates it like a drunk race-car driver at top speed. This creates a huge problem, as the only thing between my father and complete disaster is the person chasing after him. This responsibility is shared by my mother and me.

My mother is skeptical that we will be able to pull this off, but I am determined to accommodate my father's last wish. If I can talk to someone in charge, I think I can get help. I tell my parents to wait in the car.

I find two official-looking women with badges and explain, "My father is dying of brain cancer. He has days to live and he wants to vote, but I need your help. He cannot wait in line or follow a lot of rules, but if we can get him to the ballot, he is not only competent but highly intelligent and well-informed."

The kinder of the two nods empathetically and says, "If you can get him up here, I'll take care of him!"

With urgency, I push through my own limitations and my utter fatigue and try to rush back to the car where my parents are waiting. I have learned to speak in short commands when trying to be authoritative with them. "Dad, let's go!" While I focus on my father, my mother wanders off to enjoy a tiny reprieve from the exhaustive task of watching over his every waking moment.

As I try to steer my father and his walker past the long line, we hear disgruntled rumblings, "Why are they allowed to go ahead? That's not fair!"

When they get a look at my father and me staggering into the crowd, the grumbling subsides. Between the two of us, I'm sure it is hard to tell who is in worse shape.

I am frantically intervening to prevent him from crashing into people. I scream out, "I am not voting…I am just helping my father vote right now."

We finally get up to the front of the line and he shows his license and voter's card to the wonderful woman who agreed to help us. She looks at his license and then at him, then back at his license, trying to reconcile that this is the same man in the picture and asks, "Stanley, do you know what day it is?"

My father winks at me and slurs, "Nahhh, one day runs in ta the next, but I can lis the nine Supreme Court Justices in alphabetical order. Alito, Breyer…"

She interrupts him and smiles, confirming he is competent enough to vote.

Suddenly, my father announces, "I have to go to the bathroom!"

"Dad, can't it wait? We just passed everyone in line?" I sigh, exhausted.

"Jul, I gotta go," with that announcement he and his walker forge ahead of me back into the crowd. The bathroom is located behind the line, so even someone with perfect vision and balance would have to politely excuse himself as he cuts through. My father has no desire to pull this off in a civil fashion. He continues to plough through the line, ignoring the people he is knocking out of his way. After he comes out of the rest room, I pray he has his pants on. I am now forced to chase after him through the crowd to redirect him to the front of the line.

Unfortunately, the wonderful supervisor who had made the exception that allowed us to cut to the front of the line, can no longer be found. The other woman who was standing next to her when I initially explained the situation is now apparently in charge. She is demanding to see my father's identification and voter's registration card all over again. Obviously, this "Voting Nazi" has never had to take care of anyone with special needs. My father ignores her and rams his walker right past the velvet rope that is supposed to keep people in an orderly line. As she yells at us for not following the rules, I again chase after my father, trying to keep him from crashing into the voters or the booths.

I yell back at her, "He already showed you his ID! He can't follow your rules and stay behind the red line...he just wants to vote!"

She yells at us as I chase after my father, "What do you mean **my rules**? These aren't **my rules**! I need to see his identification again! You can't just cut in front of everyone else!"

*While being scolded, memories of all that my father has meant to me flood into my heart—this wonderful, quirky, funny man who taught me to love learning, reading, and politics. My father has shown me that brilliance can come in unique, messy packages, and sometimes when people are being too rigid, you just have to break the rules.*

This woman knows that he already showed ID and can see that I am completely frazzled trying to control him. I glance back at her, then ahead at my father and let him lead me to where he wants to go. This moment becomes symbolic. I have to choose. Do I behave as I am supposed to and scold my father, telling him that there are other people involved and he can't cause such a disruption, or do I just let my devotion and love for him guide me? My instincts prevail.

*Screw your unreasonable rules, it took everything this man's got left in him to get here today and vote. Sorry for the disruption, but back off and we'll be out of your way in no time.*

It was an easy choice. We push our way forward, ignoring her request to show his ID again.

Once we get to the booth, he finishes voting quickly. His mind is still sharp so he has no trouble understanding the ballot. His demeanor instantly calms as his mission is accomplished. He allows me to gently lead him out of the voting booth and through the library with no sense of urgency. As we see the "Voting Nazi" who gave us such a hard time, my father speeds up and drives the walker directly towards her. A moment of panic rushes through me as I have no idea what he is going to say or do. I don't even know if he was aware of the ordeal that he put all of us through. He approaches her and charmingly takes her hand. Just when I think he's oblivious to what occurred, he says, "I truly appreciate you accommodating me today, you are very sweet."

She melts. "You are very lucky to have such a wonderful daughter."

*Well, she certainly changed her tune. She was ready to arrest us for civil disobedience a minute ago!*

When we find my mother, she is calmly relaxing on a bench. Oblivious to our drama she asks, "Did you hear all of that commotion? It's just terrible how some people can't follow simple rules and behave in a civilized manner! Who was giving those poor volunteers such a hard time?"

My father winks at me with a devilish grin.

As we get back into the car my mother looks at me with an odd mix of worry and suspicion, "Honey, you look so exhausted!"

◄────◄────►

## November 20th 2010

My dad died today. I have some peace knowing there was nothing left unsaid between us. He had become more emotionally vulnerable at the end of his life. In fact, as a lifelong atheist, I wondered if his views were softening as he faced death.

"Hey Dad, can you give me a sign if you are okay?"

"Jul, don't look for a sign. There's not going to be any damn sign. When I die, I'm dead, that's it. There's no sign." *That's my dad! There certainly are atheists in a foxhole!*

He said two profound things to me on his deathbed. The first was, "Jul, you are the greatest pride of my life," and the second was, "Take care of your mother."

# CHAPTER 18

# Trying to Work

**January 15, 2011**

It's been three months since my father's death. When I feel up to it, I still socialize with my friends from the Lady Fit group. One of the ladies I met at the dance studio is also a cancer survivor and wants to help me. She asks if I am interested in working a few hours a week for her husband doing easy phone work. I am nervous because of my failed attempt with Susan, but I have to try.

Her husband, Peter, is a rehab specialist who evaluates whether or not people can be placed in jobs after an accident or illness. This blazing irony does not escape me.

My job is to make calls to prospective companies to see if they have job openings. Another aspect of the job is to look on employment websites searching for potential jobs that match his clients' backgrounds. This work is interesting, and I am eager to learn about the industry.

The job starts out well. I work three days a week for just two hours at a time, six hours a week, at ten bucks an hour.

Peter rarely has clients come to the office, and he's very understanding if I'm not feeling well and have to leave before my two-hour shift is complete.

*Two hours! This sounds crazy to me, particularly when I think about the days I had worked a normal eight-hour day, then attended a management meeting that could last for another three hours.*

I am able to make calls to companies fairly well, even if I have some trouble efficiently documenting the data. I can also hide many of my side effects from him because his office is located in a separate room.

After about an hour of working, my body begins to shut down. My concentration and ability to type on the computer start to deteriorate. As the two-hour mark approaches, Peter decides to teach me a new job function.

I am thinking to myself, *Oh no, I wonder if he can tell that he looks blurry? Why is the room spinning? How am I actually going to pull off that I can pay attention. He's teaching me something about putting data on a floppy disk. I am so screwed! I thought this job was just making phone calls.*

Peter doesn't realize I am not retaining anything he has tried to teach me, and he bumps my hours up to three hours a day, three times a week... *this is not an unreasonable request!*

I enthusiastically agree because I so desperately long to be "normal." I want to work up to full-time employment with benefits.

Reality has other plans...

# CHAPTER 19

# The Hospital Again?

**February 8, 2011**

I wake George up in the middle of the night. I have excruciating pain in my abdomen and I am terrified. All I can hear is the cancer specialist's office telling me, *"This kind of cancer always comes back."*

I try to numb myself with Xanax—if the cancer is back and I am going to die, why rush to the hospital? If I can just wait until the morning, I happen to have an oncology appointment with Dr. Roman tomorrow for a follow-up. George and I reluctantly agree to wait until the morning.

George drives me to my appointment. As I am checking in at the front desk, I explain that I don't feel well. The nurse takes one look at me from across the room, "You don't look well, Julie…go to the hospital immediately!"

George takes me to the hospital right next door. I am immediately admitted and a CT scan reveals a partial blockage in my lower abdomen. I'm in a holding room downstairs for a long time, waiting for a room to become available. They put a feeding tube in my nose, down my throat…OUCH… it immediately releases the pressure, and I start feeling better.

The next few days are a blur. No one is talking to me. I keep asking if I am ever going to be able to digest food again. The nurses say, "Wait for your doctor to explain things to you."

Finally! After three days of no answers, my oncologist, Dr. Roman, comes in.

I am so happy to see him, I briefly become aware of how awful I must look. My frantic questions immediately take over my vanity. "Dr. Roman, will I ever be able to eat again without a feeding tube?"

He smiles at me and calmly says, "Of course."

"Really? **Really?**"

"I am 99% sure this blockage was caused by adhesions from your surgeries. When you have a lot of scar tissue, it's not uncommon. Let's think positive and assume that was the cause. There is no way to know for sure, but if it is adhesions, the tube will eventually break it up and you should be fine. If the tube doesn't work, they may have to perform more surgery, but that's a catch 22 because more surgery means more adhesions in the future. So, we are going to try and resolve this without more surgery."

"Dr. Roman, I don't understand why no one is talking to me. You are the first one who has told me I am going to be able to eat solid food again."

He smiles compassionately at me and leans in, "Julie, they all looked at your history and wrote you off. They all assumed this was the cancer coming back."

Dr. Roman must have spoken to the hospital staff, because after his visit everyone treats me so much better. Things are going okay as long as I have the feeding tube in, but they keep taking me for scans and the blockage is still there, even though it seems to be getting smaller.

The next thing I know a hospital staff doctor appears who looks familiar. I vaguely recall him attending to me after one of my surgeries. I also remembered his arrogant demeanor and lack of bedside manner. He resembles Denzel Washington. When I was young I would have found him attractive, but now that I value kindness and empathy over a chiseled jawline, I am not so happy to see him.

He barges into my room and informs me, "The tube is coming out, but it's against my better judgment, I still see the blockage. The other doctor assigned to your case disagrees, so it has to come out."

I recall how sick I was a few days ago before they put the tube in and how painful it was to insert it. I beg him, "Can we please wait until we know it is time? I don't think it's broken up and neither do you."

He casually shrugs his shoulders, "It's not my call."

*You know those moments in your life where there is a clear junction between right and wrong? This was one of those moments.* I beg him, "**Dr. please, please**...we both know that the adhesions aren't completely broken up. You showed me on the scan that I am getting better but still blocked." I grab his arm. "Can't you fight for me?"

He coldly shrugs his shoulders and cockily repeats, "Not my call."

*Bastard!*

Soon after the tube is removed, I am brought my lunch. I have not eaten anything for days. I am assuming I will have clear broth and jello. I lift the lid to my food tray and a violent wave of nausea wafts over me. My meal looks like it should be served to someone preparing for a weightlifting competition. I am brought a full plate of heavy meat with thick brown gravy. I have rarely eaten meat since my second cancer diagnosis. I have my mom ask the nurse, "Are you sure this is what she is supposed to be eating?"

Strangely, the answer is, "Yes."

I pick at it while my mom kisses me goodbye and tells me she will be back to see me in the morning.

An hour later, I am alone in my room, projectile vomiting profusely. I manage to make it to the sink in the bathroom. The only reason someone arrives to help is that there happens to be a housekeeping staff member cleaning the room and I beg her to get me a nurse. I hear people rushing in and sounding frantic. I hear muttered voices, "She's going to aspirate, we need to get the tube back in immediately before she aspirates!"

I had two pressing questions…*Am I dying and what the hell does aspirate mean?*

When I am conscious again, I am back in my hospital bed. This young, kind doctor comes in and introduces himself to me as Dr. Zeek. He is my colon surgeon's partner.

After he reassures me that the blockage is getting better and that it just needs more time to break up, he explains that the tube has to go back in, but reiterates that I'll be just fine.

I ask him what "aspirate" means and he explains, "It means to choke on your own vomit."

As he explains this, I suddenly realize that I could have died if a member of the housecleaning staff had not been in my room when I started vomiting.

"Dr. Zeek, I have mixed feelings about the tube going back in because it hurt so much the last time."

"It hurt last time because I didn't put it in for you! I have the magic touch." He makes me laugh, glides the tube back in easily, and it hardly hurt at all. I really like him!

As I begin to realize I am not dying and that the blockage is getting better, my mood lightens and I am able to appreciate his sense of humor and light demeanor. Meanwhile, my mom rushes back to the hospital when she hears what happened. She is a very intelligent woman, but the relentless anxiety, and her age-related loss of hearing, cause her to sometimes hyper-focus on unimportant details. When she meets Dr. Zeek, he explains that a CT scan with contrast is showing the blockage is still there, but improving. For some reason, my mom hones in on the word "contrast" and keeps asking him what it means.

He answers her very calmly and patiently **the first three times.** "What it means is that the X-rays involve a contrast dye that highlights the blockage. The contrast dye itself is not an important part of the equation."

In my mother's state of anxiety, she asks **again,** "Dr Zeek… what does contrast mean?"

He clearly explains it **again** (probably thinking to himself, hmm, that's a weird thing to focus on.)

In my mom's "Xanaxed" state…taking Xanax runs in the family…she forgets she already asked what that meant, so she asks again within fifteen minutes.

It becomes a joke between the three of us, "Enough with the contrast!"

The next day he stops in to check on me. We have a friendly visit and I feel so comfortable with him in charge of my care. Before he leaves, I say to him, "Dr Zeek, I need to ask you a really serious question that I have been afraid to ask."

His sweet smile turns serious, "What is it, Julie."

"Dr. Zeek, what is contrast?" We both crack up. I consider switching to him. Would it be a viable reason to switch doctors in the same practice because one is funnier than the other one?

Things improve from here. They take me down to do a CT scan. I have to drink this thick, disgusting, milky, chalk-like barium solution. All of a sudden I am so thrilled…my stomach starts to rumble and all hell breaks loose! I know the blockage was *finally* resolved!

One of life's greatest mysteries is still left unanswered. How can I go without any food for ten days and not lose weight?

# CHAPTER 20

## Accepting the Truth

**February 21, 2011**

During my hospital stay Peter is wonderful. He and his wife send flowers and often call to check on me. I return to work a week after I get home from the hospital. I am so weak but I push myself to go to work. Peter, who had been so warm and accommodating, is showing signs he's not happy with me any longer.

Now, on top of all of my other physical limitations, I have a new debilitating problem. I can't seem to regulate my digestion. I have constant stomach cramping and sharp pains from the adhesions. Every day this week I have had to keep running to the bathroom during my two hour shift. My fatigue and concentration issues seem to have gotten worse since I was in the hospital.

When Peter tries to teach me something new, I have to write it down to remember even the simplest of tasks. Then, when he asks me to do the task, I become flustered and nervous. I know I should remember, but I just can't.

I am terrified he will ask me to do something he has tried to recently teach me. I start popping a Xanax before my work shift. My anxiety that I am messing up at this job is making the situation even worse. This is devastating. I used to be so competent!

I have managed and trained enough people in my career so I know he must be thinking, *In the time it takes me to train her, I could have done this task four times over myself!*

The inevitable happens a few weeks later. He calls me into his office and he looks so sad. He explains very nicely that he needs someone to be able to work at least four hours, three times a week. He sees that I am having trouble and feels that I should be focusing on my healing. I express that I once managed a large staff and worked over fifty hours a week. He blurts out, "**You are no longer that person!**"

This experience is humiliating. I was the golden child at every job I have ever had. I can't believe what is happening to me. He says I can work through the week and he will be happy to write a letter of recommendation. *A letter of recommendation... really? What would that say? Julie is a really nice person and kind of funny....too bad she is totally useless. Actually that's not true, on a good day, she has an hour of stamina.*

"Who is going to hire **me**?" I respond.

Fate makes my decision for me.

# CHAPTER 21

## The Dreaded Paperwork!

**March 1, 2011**

The day I get fired there is a letter in my mailbox. I finally have a date for my disability hearing! The timing of this is just too strange to ignore. I had not wanted to do this, but all roads are leading to the same destination.

In order for me to be approved for disability, my doctors have to fill out a "Residual Functional Capacity Questionnaire" form— a three-page document that rates your prognosis and ability to function in a job capacity. These questions are not things that you would normally evaluate with your doctor, such as, "Please circle the minutes your patient can sit or stand at one time," or "Will your patient need to take unscheduled breaks during an eight-hour day?

Three pages of this ...*really?* I can't even work more than an hour in an entire day. This is how they determine if I am well enough to work? I am so sick and weak, the last thing I have the energy for is to go around nagging my doctors to fill out these forms.

I drop these forms off at my primary doctor's and oncologist's offices, having discussed with them that I am applying for disability. At this point, my primary doctor delegates all of my care to Dr. Roman. My case is so complicated he won't even prescribe an aspirin without my oncologist's approval. "I will consult with your oncologist and support whatever he says," is his constant refrain.

My entire disability case is built upon my medical records and my oncologist filling out these three pages. My oncologist tells me, "I am not good at filling these forms out. Mary Jo will fill these forms out for you…she does this all the time and she is an expert."

## June 15, 2011

A month before my hearing, I give Mary Jo the forms. Right from the beginning, I have some major concerns; every time I see Mary Jo she has this confused expression like she's just finished spinning around in circles for hours. She always appears dazed, dizzy, a little confused, and unable to sustain eye contact.

I trust my oncologist, so I don't question her being in charge of my forms.

A week goes by and I haven't heard from her, so I begin to leave messages. At an oncology office, the only people you have immediate access to are chemo nurses and the main receptionist. I leave a lot of messages, bordering close to "stalker" category.

I am not physically well. I'm still having major issues as a result of the blockage and I am having trouble digesting food. I am weak and exhausted and just want to make this nightmare go away. After a week of not hearing from her, I drive to the office in a panic. My primary doctor is waiting for my oncologist to fill the forms out and then he will support what my oncologist writes…so **everything** is depending upon these damn forms.

When I get to Dr. Roman's office, I ask to speak to Mary Jo. I hear her paged several times. After waiting for close to an hour in the waiting room, she comes out to see me, frazzled as ever. I explain how important these forms are, and she asks with a smirk, "Why are you applying for disability anyway?"

I feel all the blood in my body rush to my face. *Julie, you need her. Stay calm. Stay calm.* "Mary Jo, I don't think you understand. I have no income, am uninsurable, and about to have no coverage at all. If you have any questions about why I am doing this, please talk to Dr. Roman. In the meantime I really need those forms. My hearing is coming up and my primary doctor is waiting for you to fill out the forms so he can support Dr. Roman's analysis."

She reluctantly escorts me back to her office. Oh My God! I can't believe what I am seeing. There was probably a beautiful office underneath the rubble before Mary Jo unleashed her chaos. Everywhere there are stacks and stacks of patient files to the point that many have fallen over. Folders are all over the floor and you can't even see her desk. I must confess, in my career I have been guilty of not being organized at times. I would occasionally misplace something important, but I am no match for Mary Jo. She is well within the hoarder range. Her office looks like a tsunami hit twenty minutes ago.

My heart sinks.

*I suddenly know at this moment why she hasn't called me or completed these forms…there is no way possible she could find them in this mess. My knees buckle and the wind is knocked out of me.*

*Along with the forms, I gave her an entire packet of evidence including descriptions and pictures of the intricate surgery I had, an original letter from my part-time employer showing that I cannot maintain concentration for more than two hours at a time and pages and pages of documents about my side effects and why they contribute to my case—now all lost forever in the Mary Jo rubble.*

In a panic, I try to remember if I made copies of the originals that I gave her.

Despite my anger, I regain my composure and gently make the following suggestion, hoping that I don't provoke her too much.

"Mary Jo, these are duplicates of everything I gave you, but they are all I have. How about if I leave this file with you, but please understand you cannot lose this file too, it is my entire case."

Her face distorts with rage. Her contempt for me at this moment is visible. She jumps down my throat, completely offended by my insinuation. "I haven't lost anything!"

I wanted to ask her to make a copy of these documents I am handing her, but I realize that's out of the question!

I leave, feeling utterly exhausted, depressed, and depleted. I go home and crash for days, unable to get out of bed. The clock is ticking. My hearing is now less than a week away. My lawyer's office is calling me, relentlessly asking, "Where are the documents? Where are the documents? You can't go to court without these documents!"

I leave another message on Mary Jo's voice mail:

"Hi, Mary Jo, this is Julie Klein. I really need those papers as my hearing is days away. I am coming to the office and will wait in the lobby until they are ready."

I do not hear back from her, so I pack enough food to sustain me for the entire day and drive to Dr. Roman's office. I am prepared to sit in the waiting room all day until the papers are done. To my surprise, Mary Jo comes out immediately and calmly says, "They will be ready tomorrow, I promise."

The next day, prepared for battle, I drive back to the office again. It is now just three days before my hearing. Surprisingly, the papers are ready! Now I just have to give these papers to my primary doctor so he can fill in his portion supporting Dr. Roman's documentation. I am ready for a straight jacket!

# CHAPTER 22

# Disability Hearing

**July 14, 2011**

Ironically, I feel relief as I am getting dressed for my Disability hearing today. For the past several years I have been trying desperately hard to protect the people that love me by pretending to be stronger and healthier than I really am. I am exhausted from trying to be better, to be someone I no longer am, to be Julie before cancer. It is liberating to not have to pretend any longer. I can allow myself to appear sick in front of the world...no wig, no blush, no cute shoes that burn my feet and are excruciating to wear.

At 9:00 a.m my friend, Susan picks me up and we drive downtown to where the hearing is being held. There's an information desk and rest-room on the first floor. We ask where disability hearings are held and an older gentleman behind the desk looks at me knowingly, directing me to the 15th floor.

Conversations can be overheard in the elevator that in other circumstances may not have any meaning, "I can't tell if it went in my favor," or "I really lost my cool in there." Despite my nervousness, as I glance around I can't help but notice some of the other scared, pale faces with dead eyes.

When we reach the 15th floor, there's a sign on the door that leads us to another check-in desk where we have to show ID and allow our purses to be searched. We also have to go through airport-style security scanners. I show my driver's license at another window; Susan is escorted to the waiting room where I join her after signing in.

The waiting room at a disability hearing is a fascinating place to spend the morning if you aren't facing one of the most nerve-wracking experiences of your life.

It's a strange and dark mix of lost human souls. Across from me is a war veteran who had been shot multiple times, was exposed to Agent Orange, and clearly suffers from some type of residual post-traumatic stress. Next to him is a frail, anorexic-looking woman who reeks of alcohol and slurs her words. There are others in the waiting room who look close to normal, although no one exactly appears as if they are there for a job interview. The attorneys, however, are easy to recognize in their polished suits with wheeled brief cases that they cart like luggage.

I have not met my attorney before today, a fact that does not sit well with me because my case has been pending for two years. Somehow, he knows who I am.

"Ms. Klein, I am your attorney, Kevin..." I don't catch his last name but I like him immediately. He's confident without being cocky. He's young enough to be hungry, but old enough to be good at what he does. Perfect!

We spoke for the first time yesterday over the phone and I bombarded him with questions. He interrupted me and said, "Slow down! I have all of your medical records in front of me and I have this under control."

"Kevin, you have to understand something. I have so much riding on this. I can no longer support myself and this is my only way to have any income and obtain medical insurance. I hadn't spoken with you before today. I have been so worried about my case but now that we have talked, I feel much better so I am going to calm down, and trust you."

Upon meeting Kevin in person, we click immediately. He takes me into a prep room and goes over a few last minute details. He never tells me what to say or not to say.

"If you want to break me and cause me to cry, ask me why I can't support myself any longer." I start to go off on an emotional tangent, "I've been through two cancers and multiple invasive surgeries, but you want to know what I can't handle? I can't handle not being able to work anymore and… "

Kevin stops me and touches my hand, "Julie, I know. I've been doing this a long time and I know what type of person you are. Don't go there now, save it for the judge so your emotion is raw. I am going to hit you hard on this." I am so impressed with him. *He gets me. He finds my "Achilles heel" in less than an hour. Wow, he's good!*

I am now relatively calm after meeting Kevin and taking another Xanax. We walk into a small, barren conference room. Kevin directs me to a chair closest to the door. I sit facing the judge who's slightly elevated on a platform. Kevin sits to my left. A very serious, well-dressed man sits to Kevin's left. He is the vocational specialist who will determine if I can be retrained. I believe there's a court reporter in the room on the other side of me, but I am so focused on everyone else that I don't remember if the person is young or old, or male or female.

The Judge reads some instructions and swears me in. My attorney makes a flawless opening statement, attesting to my character and the fact that I did not file immediately when I was unable to work. He explains that I tried multiple part-time jobs beneath my educational level after my illness. He then succinctly and accurately describes the medical events of the past few years.

Then the testimony begins. I expect to be asked questions by everyone in the room, but only my lawyer addresses me:

"Tell me about your work background."

"Tell me about your most recent job with Mr. Collins."

"Tell me about your breast cancer treatments."

"Then what happened," leading me to talk about my second cancer.

I reply, "This diagnosis was devastating. After just finishing a year and a half of treatment for stage three, aggressive breast cancer, I am immediately diagnosed with an aggressive stage 3 appendix cancer."

"Did the breast cancer spread?"

"No, the second cancer was a new primary tumor."

"Tell me more about this second cancer."

"It is an extremely rare, aggressive cancer of the appendix. At first, it was misdiagnosed as an ovarian cyst. They did not know they were dealing with cancer when I had it removed, so precautions were not taken to prevent the spread of cancer cells. When the pathology came back a week later and my doctors realized this was a rare, aggressive cancer, there was much concern and debate over how to properly treat this. Apparently, there are cancer cells that can escape during the surgery and form new aggressive tumors. It was explained to me that I could possibly be facing constant 'debulking' surgeries for the rest of my life, continuously removing tumor after tumor until I eventually die of the disease, which is probably only 2-3 years from now.

"So how did they end up treating this?"

"My doctors were not in agreement. One doctor strongly believed my only chance for survival was to have something called a "Hot Chemo Wash" which basically boils your organs to kill any remaining cancer cells. The surgeon I went with felt this was way too harsh for me, considering I was already in a weakened immune state from the first cancer. I ended up having major surgery to remove 1/3 of my colon, followed by six months of aggressive chemo which has left me with a lot of permanent neurological damage. I have had a total of 32 rounds of chemo. When I asked my oncologist if I will ever recover and feel normal again, he replied, 'Julie, you have had enough chemo to kill an elephant.'

"How were you after the surgery?"

"My surgeon took 17 lymph nodes and multiple biopsies. Luckily, there was no sign that the cancer had spread. However, the surgery was very extensive and has caused chronic stomach problems."

"Tell me about how your stomach surgeries have affected your life."

"There are two types of pain that I experience. One is a sharp, quick-stabbing sensation, those are from the adhesions. More concerning are the cramp-like symptoms that can last for hours. This is scarier because I could be constipated and this may lead to another blockage. A few months ago I was hospitalized for a week because I had a blockage from the scar tissue. This time they were able to break it up by inserting a feeding tube down my nose. My oncologist told me that if I get another blockage I will need to have more surgery. I have already told my surgeon, "Don't wake me up if I need a bag to live"

*I look at the judge head on, I need to relay to her that I am not making this up!*

Kevin's sense of timing is perfect and relentless, "Are you able to sleep, Ms. Klein?"

"I can be dead tired but the moment my body relaxes and I lay down, I get a hot flash from the drug I am on to prevent the breast cancer from coming back and my heart palpitates, then my mind starts to race. I hear the words in my head from one of the cancer experts I had consulted, 'This kind of cancer always comes back,' and that's what I go to bed thinking about every night." *My eyes are still locked with the judge's.*

"Tell me about your neuropathy."

"Neuropathy is a weird thing to describe. I either can't feel my hands and feet or they prick like I am being stabbed with pins and needles. I have to give myself monthly B-12 shots because the part of my colon that was removed is the part that absorbs B-12. This temporarily seems to help the neuropathy but about a week before the month is up, my hand starts to clench like this, *I make a lobster claw-like gesture,* and I can't control my dexterity."

All of a sudden there is an outburst from the judge. Her hand flies up in the air and she pleads that I stop talking.

"**I've heard enough.**" She looks at my lawyer and says "**January, 2008**."

She then looks at me and says, "I wish you well, Ms. Klein."

Kevin escorts me out of the room.

"I'm so confused! What happened in there? When will I know how it went? What did she mean when she said January 2008?"

"Julie, you won."

"What? Are you sure? Everything happened so quickly."

"Yes, Julie, you won."

I stop in the middle of the hallway and turn to Kevin. I make no attempt to hide the tears of gratitude flooding down my face. "How do I ever thank you? You understood **everything**. You spoke so well on my behalf."

"**You** did it, Julie. You were honest about what you went through and your case speaks for itself. The judge approved your disability from the first date you couldn't work, which means you are immediately eligible for medicare.

Then the enormity of it all hits me:

*no more fear of becoming indigent after working my entire life… no more ongoing panic that I can no longer hold down a job and support myself… no more relentless terror that I will have to go through my life savings due to medical costs…no more hours, days, and weeks on the phone trying unsuccessfully to find affordable, decent health care with two pre-existing cancers…in an instant, with a flick of the judge's hand…I am vindicated.*

*I can finally breathe and begin to rebuild the best quality of life I can for myself.*

**I did it…I survived!**